CESJ PARADIGM PAPER

— THE —
RESTORATION
OF PROPERTY

—

A Reexamination of a Natural Right

By

Michael D. Greaney, CPA, MBA

Director of Research

Center for Economic and Social Justice

Economic Justice Media

Published by Economic Justice Media, an imprint of CESJ
P. O. Box 40711, Washington, D.C. 20016, U.S.A.
(Tel) 703-243-5155 • (Fax) 703-243-5935
(Eml) thirdway@cesj.org • (Web) www.cesj.org

International Standard Book Number: 978-0-944997-07-9

Library of Congress Control Number: 2010907142

Cover design by Rowland L. Brohawn

Table of Contents

The author would like to acknowledge the invaluable assistance of Dr. Norman G. Kurland, president of the Center for Economic and Social Justice, and Dawn K. Brohawn, CESJ's Director of Communications, in the preparation of this monograph. Any errors that remain are my own, and the opinions expressed do not necessarily represent the views of Dr. Kurland, Ms. Brohawn, or the official position of CESJ.

1. Introduction

If only because power naturally and necessarily follows property, concentrated ownership of the means of production is the most serious political and economic problem in the world today. People as diverse as Karl Marx and Pope John Paul II have viewed this "ownership gap" as a root cause of fundamental social problems. It is, as well, a result of flawed and unjust laws and institutions. These, in turn, create flagrant inequalities of economic opportunity and personal freedom. A social order that systematically concentrates economic power must therefore be viewed as an explicit offense against human dignity. The question becomes what to do about it.

In response, in 1936 Hilaire Belloc published *An Essay on the Restoration of Property.*[1] His concern was that a society characterized by the lack of widespread, direct ownership of the means of production — capital — is a sick society, one contrary to human nature, and thus ill-suited to providing the proper environment within which human beings can become more fully themselves.

If society continued on its then course of increasingly concentrated ownership of the means of production in either a private elite or the hands of the State — and recall that Belloc was writing in 1936 — the social order would devolve in one of two ways. One, capitalist economies would transform themselves into the "Servile State." Belloc described this in his 1912 book of the same title. Two, socialism, especially in its most aggravated form, communism, would be instituted in an effort to alleviate the problems caused by concentrated private ownership of the means of production by abolishing private property and making the State the ultimate owner of everything.

---

[1] New York: Sheed and Ward, 1936.

What Belloc failed to mention was the fact that the Servile State as he described it — really, the socialization of capitalism, so well implemented by the virtually global adherence to Keynesian economics — is, in its final stages, the transformation of private capitalism into State capitalism: socialism. The private elite of capitalism and the public elite of socialism merge their interests and for all practical purposes become indistinguishable.

Nor are the other major schools of economics, the Monetarist and the Austrian, any antidote to the Servile State and the ultimate transformation of capitalism into socialism. The Monetarist and the Austrian schools, operating from within a morally deficient paradigm — blind and indifferent to institutional causes of the ownership gap — are merely attempts to maintain capitalism in palatable form. This is an effort doomed to failure. Whatever their economic theories might tell them, a propertyless majority is politically — and financially — unstable, and contrary to essential human nature.

Paralleling Aristotle's paradox about democratic behavior not always being the best or most effective way to maintain democracy,[2] maintaining capitalism requires that capitalism be modified for its own survival. Capitalists will necessarily transform capitalism into the Servile State because they must incorporate social programs to take care of those perceived as less fortunate, and at the same time institute political aims and goals to maintain current power structures. The alternative is economic collapse due to insufficient demand to keep the economy running, or political overthrow of the ruling elite by the propertyless masses.

This is consistent with Walter Bagehot's analysis in *The English Constitution* (1867), and *Lombard Street* (1873). These are works that, while purporting to support democracy and capitalism, incorporate the totalitarian philosophy of Thomas Hobbes as detailed in *Leviathan* (1651), often considered a work whose premises justify socialism.

---

[2] *The Politics*, V.v.

In *The English Constitution*, Bagehot redefined "democracy" to mean rule of the British Empire by an economic elite, the financial and commercial classes of England. This was through these elites' control of the House of Commons, running the Empire as a private business venture. In *Lombard Street: A Description of the Money Market*, Bagehot explained how the financial and commercial elites control the economy for their private benefit. They based economic control on the redefinition of money put forth by the British Currency School and embodied in Sir Robert Peel's Bank Charter Act of 1844.[3] The ideal arrangement was that imposed by the British East India Company on the Indian subcontinent, and which came crashing down with the Great Mutiny of 1857.

Where Bagehot made his case that this arrangement of the political and economic orders is all for the best, if not ideal, Belloc described the same situation in *The Servile State*, but took the opposite position. Belloc concluded that, "the tendency to the reestablishment of slavery as a necessary development of capitalism is patent wherever capitalism has power."[4]

Capitalism transforms itself into the Servile State out of sheer necessity. The process involves making the great mass of people completely dependent on the elite for a wage system job, or on State programs instituted to redistribute wealth — often both at the same time. This dependency can be imposed directly through the implicit or explicit abolition of private property and implementation of the wage system. Alternatively, dependency can be imposed indirectly through the manipulation of monetary and fiscal policy for private or political ends, or via artificial job creation programs that are simply a more complicated and wasteful form of redistribution.

Similarly, socialism must inevitably implement what is often vaguely called "free market reforms." Socialist

---

[3] Vict. 7 & 8, c. 32.
[4] Hilaire Belloc, *The Servile State*. Indianapolis, Indiana: Liberty Fund, Inc., 1977, 35.

economies must add a veneer of capitalism in order to gain the somewhat dubious advantage of the restricted exercise of normal and healthy self-interest by a pre-selected elite. Those in charge of the socialist economy thereby hope to gain the ephemeral benefits of controlled competition and a limited profit motive.

At the same time, the vast majority of people remain trapped in a condition of utter dependency and unable to participate in the "new" economy except as subsidized labor and limited consumers. Even in those cases in which a socialist economy officially transforms into a capitalist economy, there is an inevitable backlash and a demand for a return to socialism as the cure for the capitalism that was implemented as the remedy for socialism . . . .

Small wonder that Belloc's *Restoration of Property* is a grim effort that ultimately offers nothing practicable as a solution — as Belloc admitted in his Preface:

It is customary in presenting any political thesis to include an element of hope. Professional politicians always make a point of prophesying success and even more respectable and sincere reformers love to exaggerate the changes of their ideal and even to affirm its ultimate victory as certain.

This has always seemed to me great folly. Wisdom consists in the appreciation of reality. If you approach a most difficult task under the illusion or the pretence that it is less difficult you may strengthen your supporters by the drug of illusion but you weaken them much more by persuading them to work in the void.

Respect for reality compels me to say that the Restoration of Property when that institution has all but disappeared is a task *almost* impossible of achievement. If it were *quite* impossible of achievement it would not be worth while wasting breath or ink upon it. It is not *quite* impossible of achievement; at least, it is not quite impossible to start the beginnings of a change. But the odds against a reconstruction of economic freedom in a society which has long acquired the practice and habit of wage slavery is difficult beyond any other political task.[5]

Keep in mind that these words were written three-quarters of a century ago, and the situation has, if anything, gotten much worse than Belloc ever appeared to imagine or fear. The degree of economic, social, and legal dependency so contrary to a morally just market economy has increased to the point where the powerless condition is not only accepted, most people — especially our leaders and policymakers (to say nothing of academics) — consider it normal.

Evidently we can neither move forward nor stay where we are. The only solution seen by many, including Belloc, is to dismantle modern civilization. They believe they can make civilization more manageable by reducing it down to a more "human scale." Is there, however, a reasonable alternative consistent with human nature? A just third way above and beyond both capitalism and socialism, and that does not require us to regress to subsistence farming, artisan crafts, or hunting and gathering? (It is notable that the strongest advocates of the "small is beautiful" approach have rarely, if ever, been absolutely dependent on subsistence agriculture or handicrafts to meet their own consumption needs.) We believe that there is, in fact, a "Just Third Way" that does not require we sacrifice centuries of progress in order to force everyone down to the same level of misery. This requires a better understanding of power and property.

Unfortunately, these days "power" is a dirty word, and "property" is well on its way to becoming one, even among distributists, adherents of a system developed by Belloc and G. K. Chesterton based on widespread ownership of capital. This is hardly surprising, when we consider Daniel Webster's dictum that "power naturally and necessarily follows property." In the United States, a country explicitly founded on the belief in the sovereignty and personhood of each and every human being, and the idea that

---

[5] *The Restoration of Property, op. cit.*, 11-12.

the State derives all of its powers from "We, the People," matters have reached such a pitch that even the United States Supreme Court bestows and withholds personality, apparently when and where it will.

This has the effect of making every citizen a "mere creature of the State,"[6] whether we are referring to outright socialism, or the Servile State as a kind of halfway house on the road to complete State control. People lose sight of the fact that the State — by its nature and function society's only tolerable monopoly — must be limited to its proper role as a very specialized social tool charged with the care and maintenance of the common good. This the State does best and most consistently with the Just Third Way by limiting its economic operations, policing abuses, and providing a level playing field as a government of the people, by the people, and for the people — not an economic or State elite.

As Belloc noted, the State best cares for the common good by providing an opportunity for ordinary people to become owners of the means of production, and in maintaining the order necessary to a stable social order. As he stated,

> There must exist in some form the State. A sufficiently large unit for the development of the arts and the better complexities of life must be organised. Its power must be appealed to for the satisfaction of justice, the prevention of internal disorder and for the arrangement of defence against external aggression. In general the State must exercise some restraint upon the ideal economic freedom of the family or freedom itself cannot be guaranteed.[7]

In other words, "property" does not mean doing what you will with what you own. On the contrary (as is the case with democracy itself) true economic freedom consists of limiting the exercise of your rights of private property in order to maintain your absolute right to be an

---

[6] See *Pierce v. Society of Sisters*, 268 U.S. 510 1925.

[7] *The Restoration of Property*, op. cit., 15-16.

owner within the common good. In short, you cannot use your possessions to harm yourself or others, or the common good as a whole. This is how we can speak of each human being having an absolute right *to* private property, but limited rights *of* private property . . . as long as the exercise of private property is not defined in any way that undermines the absolute — natural, inherent, inalienable — right to be an owner in the first place.

As one of the founders of the distributist movement, Belloc recognized the fact that widespread ownership of the means of production is essential to a healthy society. This is consistent with the natural moral law. As he said, defining "economic freedom" as ownership of an adequate stake of income-generating assets, "Economic freedom can only be a good if it fulfils some need in our nature."[8] He first explained why private property is important. He then presented a general program for achieving the goal of expanded capital ownership.

From the first there were serious problems with Belloc's proposals. This is not surprising given the grimness of his outlook — and, unfortunately, given his definition of money. This, ironically, is the same as Bagehot and Keynes, a definition contrary to the natural moral law, as we will see in subsequent chapters. Not the least of these was the paradox that Belloc proposed measures that he did not believe could be successful or would work in the current state of society. This, in and of itself, is contrary to social justice.

It is a basic characteristic of social justice as discerned by the Reverend William J. Ferree, S.M., Ph.D., that whatever actions we propose to effect necessary changes in the social order must be *effective*.[9] As "political animals," humanity is, obviously, being most consistent with human nature when acting *politically*. Politics being the art of the *possible*, we should never waste our time trying

---

[8] *Ibid.*, 21.
[9] *Introduction to Social Justice*. Arlington, Virginia: Center for Economic and Social Justice, 1997, 51-52.

to accomplish something that, however virtuous we may believe it to be, we have already decided is *impossible*. Instead, our efforts must be directed to organizing with like-minded others so that barriers that prevent full participation in the economic common good can be eliminated, not raised.

Then (while this was obviously not Belloc's intent) it was clear that the remedy he proposed is manifestly contrary to justice. That is, he advocated imposing disabilities on the rich to bring them down to the level of the poor, rather than lifting barriers that prevent the poor from participating in the economy on the same terms as the rich. Obviously, something that calls itself the Just Third Way necessarily rejects anything that relies on injustice to achieve its ends.

Belloc's proposed solution would have imposed barriers instead of eliminating them. Nevertheless, imposing limits on the exercise of rights within the common good is, despite the modern tendency to confuse barriers and limits, not contrary to justice. Laws, customs, traditions, and so on, impose limitations all the time in order properly to define the exercise of humanity's natural rights. While natural rights are inalienable, that is, each human being has the full spectrum of such natural rights as life, liberty, property, and the pursuit of happiness inherent in his or her being as a part of human nature, no one may exercise his or her rights, however absolutely held, in any way that harms another individual, a group, or the common good as a whole — or even him- or herself.

Belloc had it backwards. He was right that the rich enjoy financial advantages to which the poor do not have access. The poor suffer harm through their inability to gain equal access to the means of acquiring and possessing private property: money and credit. The proper course of action, however, is not to inflict harm on the rich to make them "equal" to the poor. Two wrongs do not make a right. Such a program partakes not of justice, but of revenge. Neither can we change the definition of natural rights such as life, liberty, and property in order to justify imposing limits on some, but not on others, or abolishing a right as part of the natural law.

Instead, the financial institutions of society must be restructured to open up democratic access to money and credit, the most effective means for non-owners to become owners of wealth-producing assets. Only then will the poor have an equal opportunity with everyone else to become rich. The idea is not that the rich should be made poor, or forced to pay for presumed crimes against humanity when they have broken no human law, but that the poor should have the same opportunities as previously enjoyed exclusively by the rich.

Ultimately, the goal of the Just Third Way is to establish and maintain an economically just society. We can define an economically just society as one that meets four essential "pillars" that uphold and protect the dignity of the human person. These four pillars are:

1. **A limited economic role for the State**. The State is a specialized tool (as we have already stressed, a legitimate monopoly) designed to assist humanity in caring for and maintaining the common good. Only in extreme cases or for expedience can we justify using the State to care for and maintain individual goods. The State's role should be limited to providing a "level playing field," enforcing contracts, and policing abuses. The State should function only by consent of its citizens and be economically dependent on the people, rather than forcing a condition of dependency by attempting to provide for each individual's wants and needs.

2. **Free and open markets within a fair and understandable system of laws as the best means for determining just wages, just prices, and just profits**. Humanity's natural right of liberty — free association — means that people should be free and un-coerced either by other individuals or groups, or conditions, to use their personal judgment within an open and free market system to determine democrati-

cally the value of their labor, their capital, and the marketable goods and services produced by means of their labor and their capital stakes.

3. **Restoration of the rights of private property, especially in corporate equity**. The business corporation, a legally recognized expression of humanity's freedom of association, while designed to make it possible for many people to own jointly a single asset and make the enjoyment of ownership of the means of production more widespread, has been used to concentrate ownership and restrict and in some cases abolish the rights of minority owners to control their proportionate share of governance powers and other fruits of ownership, such as their just share of the income.

4. **Widespread direct ownership of capital**. This "pillar" can be regarded as the fatal omission of every economic system in the world today — and the one Belloc directly addressed, although inadequately and with a faulty understanding of the institutions of money and credit.

It is all very well, of course, to say that we want an economically just society, and that an economically just society consists of the four pillars. Nevertheless, despite our great desire, even our need to establish what Belloc variously calls the Proprietary or Distributist State, we must not, indeed, *cannot* do it by means that contradict the goal itself. We cannot, for instance, take what belongs to one simply because we wish to give it to another. We would thereby destroy property for some for the benefit of others — and make all property insecure in the process. Nor can we change the meaning of "property" in order to achieve the form of our goal but without the substance.

And what is the substance? Belloc himself accurately identified that. As he said (and keep in mind that "ownership" and "control" are the same in all codes of law), "It is obvious that whoever controls the means of production controls the supply of wealth. If, therefore, the means for the production of that wealth which a family needs are in the control of others than the family, the family will be dependent upon those others; it will not be economically free."[10]

Therefore, in contrast to many so-called proposals today, whose proponents assert that people should just not be greedy and should share what they have, the Just Third Way does not go against human nature. Instead, the Just Third Way is designed to act in conformity with human nature, that is, with the natural moral law. That means such inalienable rights as life, liberty, property, and the pursuit of happiness, based as they are on human nature, cannot be ignored or circumvented. Further, humanity being "political" by nature (a combination of individual and social), it makes no sense just to give orders without working to reform our social structures to make doing the right thing optimal or even possible.

For that reason, we have developed an outline for a possible program that we believe contains the essential elements of a specific program that will 1) restructure some basic institutions, in order to 2) make specific actions possible. We have arranged these points in what we think is the proper order, but that depends on what becomes possible and when we can do it. It is not a pre-determined rigid program from which we cannot deviate. Also, being human, we may have left something off of the list.

1. Accelerate Private Sector Growth

In order to encourage private sector growth in which all citizens, not just a select few, participate on an equal basis with respect to opportunity, we propose that all dividends be made fully tax deductible at the corporate level, although fully taxable as ordinary income at the personal level. This is because existing accumulations will no longer be necessary to serve as collateral for financing new capital formation. Existing savings can be put to use funding consumer demand (including housing loans), and high-risk ventures, and speculation in securities, without

---

[10] *The Restoration of Property, op. cit.*, 14.

induced inflation or redistribution through the tax system. This would, in and of itself, provide the basis for a sound economy in which production and consumption income are equalized, and the economy operates without State interference or manipulation.

2. Reform the Myth of Savings

Virtually all economists and policymakers today have the fixed belief that the only way to finance capital formation, that is, to invest in new income-generating assets, is to cut consumption, save, then invest. This assumption is utterly false, as was proved by Dr. Harold G. Moulton in his 1935 classic, *The Formation of Capital*. Louis O. Kelso and Mortimer J. Adler integrated Moulton's findings into a sound program of economic reform in their book, *The New Capitalists* (1961). The subtitle of Kelso and Adler's book sums up the goal in the most succinct manner possible: "A Proposal to Free Economic Growth from the Slavery of Savings" — meaning *past*, not *future* savings.

3. Reform the Money and Credit System

The fundamental change needed in our money and credit system is to correct our understanding of "money." Money is not restricted to State sanctioned or authorized legal tender. Instead, money is anything — repeat *anything* — that can be used in settlement of a debt. If we assume that only the State can issue or authorize money, we *necessarily* assume total State control over the economy, and thus the imposition of a condition of dependency on every citizen, making each one "a mere creature of the State" — socialism. As Meyer Anselm Rothschild is reputed to have said, "Give me control of a nation's money, and I care not who makes the laws."[11]

4. Own the Fed

If State control over money and credit through the wrong definition of money leads to socialism, permitting a private elite to control money and credit through the same

---

[11] Frederick Merton, *The Rothschilds, A Family Portrait*, New York: Atheneum, 1962.

means leads to the Servile State — the same destination by two different routes. Thus, in contrast to proposals that call for the abolition of the Federal Reserve System, or turning it over to the direct control of the federal government, we advocate putting the "money power" in the hands of the people most concerned with it: every citizen, as a shared right of citizenship. The proper functioning of a central bank is as a unique social tool. This tool cannot, without grave consequences to individual goods and the common good, be controlled by either a private or a public elite. We propose that every citizen and legal resident in the region served by the Federal Reserve directly own the Federal Reserve. This would be via a single, no-cost, lifetime, non-transferable, voting share in the regional Federal Reserve Bank in the district in which the citizen maintains his or her primary residence or home of record. Through the rights of private property, this would make the money power more directly accountable to the people, and eliminate what some have called "a despotic economic dictatorship."[12] The net result would be a transformation of a nation's central bank into something like or analogous to a "fourth branch of government," but controlled and operated directly by the people.

5. Reform the Tax System

The national tax system in the United States is a national disgrace. The tax code is gargantuan. No one person can claim to understand the Internal Revenue Code, or even a single section of the Code. That being the case, it makes sense to simplify the system — but only if it can be done in a just and fair manner. We must first keep in mind that the goal of the tax system is to raise the revenue necessary for the proper functioning of the State, not social engineering, or to bolster the power of whatever elite happens to be in charge at the moment. We propose, therefore, to eliminate most deductions, increase the exemption and limited deductions for non-dependents to

---

[12] Pius XI, *Quadragesimo Anno* ("On the Restructuring of the Social Order"), 1931, § 105.

$30,000, for dependents to $20,000, eliminate the payroll tax, merge all taxes into a single rate levied on all income (and we mean *all* income) above the extremely generous exemption level, and set the single rate at a level sufficient to meet all current government expenditures from general revenues, including all promised Social Security, Medicare, and other entitlements, and pay down the national debt within a reasonable period of time.

6. Enact a Capital Homestead Act

The goal is to restore private property "in a Society which has almost forgotten what property and its concomitant freedom means."[13] Following the lead of Abraham Lincoln's 1862 Homestead Act, a Capital Homestead Act would justly and rapidly open up equal opportunity for every man, woman, and child in America to acquire an equal share of the approximately $2 trillion of new, productive capital formed each year in the United States. This would not be inflationary, because the money needed to acquire the new capital would not be created until and unless a financially feasible capital project was located and properly vetted by local commercial banks. Money can be created as needed without inflation by discounting and rediscounting private sector bills of exchange. This links the new money through private property directly to the present value of existing and future marketable goods and services. New money is *only* created in direct response to and in no greater amount than the present value of new capital formation and existing inventories.[14] Every citizen would use an equal allocation of nonrecourse capital credit to acquire capital, repay the loan with the income generated by the capital itself, and collateralize the loan with capital credit insurance paid for out of the "risk premium" typically charged and pooled on all loans.

---

[13] *The Restoration of Property, op. cit.,* 144.
[14] This is the "real bills doctrine," an application of "Say's Law of Markets." All three mainstream schools of economics reject the real bills doctrine, and reject or redefine Say's Law of Markets.

This is the barest outline of what needs to be done. In subsequent chapters in this book we will examine each of the four pillars and the programmatic points in greater detail. By this means we will overcome the unfortunate weaknesses inherent in Belloc's proposal to restore private property, while at the same time not violate any of our essential principles.

2. Accelerate Private Sector Growth

Before we begin in earnest, we need to list some of the specific ways in which the financial and tax systems need to be restructured in order to accelerate private sector economic growth. Our overall approach — the philosophy — is something we call the "Just Third Way." The specific application we advocate is called "Capital Homesteading." The Just Third Way requires a dramatic paradigm shift, especially in our understanding of money.

On the economic level with which we are concerned, the Just Third Way requires that we shift from the tenets of the British Currency School, to those of the British Banking School. Adherence to the principles underlying the Currency School understanding of money has hampered, even prevented sound economic growth for centuries. While not perfect, the principles on which the Banking School is based are more consistent with economic and political reality than the contradictory assumptions and dictates of the Currency School.

In brief, the Currency School claims that "money" consists of coin, banknotes, and demand deposits, along with selected time deposits. That is, "money" (as John Maynard Keynes asserted) is whatever the State says it is.[1] This necessarily requires that financing for new capital formation can only come out of cutting consumption and accumulating unconsumed production in the form of money savings.[2]

---

[1] John Maynard Keynes, *A Treatise on Money, Volume I: The Pure Theory of Money*. New York: Harcourt, Brace and Company, 1930, 4.

[2] Harold G. Moulton, *Capital Expansion, Employment, and Economic Stability*. Washington, DC: The Brookings Institution, 1940, 26.

The Banking School claims that "money" is anything that can be accepted in settlement of a debt. Consistent with Say's Law of Markets, money is simply a symbol of the present value of existing and future marketable goods and services in which the issuer of the money has a private property stake. The State's role is limited to setting the standard of whatever is used as money, enforcing contracts when some dispute arises, and generally ensuring as far as possible a "level playing field."

In other words, money is a contract. Issuing something to be used as money does not make something money. It is only an "offer." It is not until another party *accepts* the offer that a contract — money — exists. A government can issue as much paper as it likes, backing it with an iron-clad promise — its "full faith and credit" — to make good on the obligation out of future tax revenues, but if no one accepts the paper, it is not money.

The belief that the mere issuing something as money constitutes "money creation" pervades modern thinking about money, credit, banking and finance. This has only succeeding in creating massive confusion about what constitutes just monetary and fiscal policy. No one was more confused about this aspect of money than John Maynard Keynes, the architect of the modern global economy.

Many of today's economists assert that Keynes was not Currency School, but Banking School.[3] This is based on a misunderstanding of Say's Law and the real bills doctrine. To oversimplify somewhat, Say's Law is that money is the medium by means of which we trade what we produce for what others produce — enter into contracts — and how we store the value of what we produce until we exchange it for the productions of others. Thus (as Say's Law is often misleadingly stated), supply generates its own demand, and demand its own supply, or (even more simply), production equals income.

---

[3] *Vide, e.g.*, Charles P. Kindleberger, *Manias, Panics, and Crashes: A History of Financial Crises*. New York: Harper Collins, Publishers, 1989, 60.

The real bills doctrine is that the quantity of money can be decreased or increased as required without inflation or deflation of the currency. Three conditions are required for the real bills doctrine to operate. One, the quantity of money must not exceed the present value of existing and future marketable goods and services in the economy. Two, the issuer of the money must have a private property stake in the present value of the existing and future marketable goods and services that back the money. Three — and keep in mind that this is the only thing that actually makes something "money" — the issuer's offer must be *accepted*; only acceptance of a tender offer makes something truly "money."

Keynes rejected both Say's Law and the real bills doctrine. It is thus incorrect to claim that Keynes was "Banking School" simply because he advocated manipulating the currency through the central bank. Keynes's approach necessarily tied economic growth, even ownership of the means of production, irrevocably to existing accumulations of savings, whether it remained under the control of private interests, or control (and thus effective ownership) is assumed by the State. This artificially constrains economic growth and prevents most people from ever owning anything other than consumer goods, or a token amount of equity in capital goods. It assumes insufficiency or scarcity as inevitable.

Consequently, we need to reject the artificial scarcity constraints built into the Currency School approach by the Reverend Thomas Malthus and others. This requires that we revive and restore the real bills doctrine and Say's Law of Markets. To accomplish the goal of an economically just society, we believe that a Capital Homesteading program should focus primarily on increasing production by accelerating democratic growth of the private sector. This would be effective if for no other reason than making new investments productive and making certain the income from ownership is distributed widely and, above all, *equitably* throughout society in accordance with the principles of economic justice will ensure as far as humanly possible a sound and sustainable economic recovery.

The Just Third Way as applied in Capital Homesteading is the only rational alternative to capitalism, socialism, or a diluted distributism corrupted into effective socialism by a bad definition of money and reliance on existing accumulations of savings to finance capital formation. A Capital Homestead Act offers the following goals in place of Belloc's unfortunate (and seemingly completely unconscious) Statism:

Promote Private Sector Growth Linked to Broadened Ownership. Recreate in the 21st century the conditions that resulted from Abraham Lincoln's 1862 Homestead Act. As a Capital Homestead Act would be based on all productive capital, not just land, this would include full employment, declining prices, and widespread, individual and effective ownership of income generating assets. Part of the Act would be to set a realistic long-term target, based on the nation's industrial growth potential. The goal would be to achieve a minimum Capital Homestead stake for every American family within a reasonable period of time.

Stimulate Maximum Growth, with a Balanced Budget and Zero Inflation Rate. Remove barriers to maximum rates of sustainable and environmentally sound, private sector growth to achieve a balanced federal budget, and a zero inflation rate under a Capital Homestead program.

Establish a Tax System That Stimulates Economic Growth and Jobs, and is More Accountable to Taxpayers. Rewrite and radically simplify the existing federal tax system to automatically balance the budget. Keep more money in the pockets of taxpayers from their initial earnings to cover their own health, education, housing and other basic household living expenses. Make Congress more directly accountable and responsive to all taxpayers. Eliminate all tax provisions, personal deductions, tax credits, and exemptions (except for the front-end ex-

emptions for adults and dependents) that unjustly
discriminate against or discourage property accumulations and investment incomes for poor and non-rich
families.

**Keep the Social Security System and Medicare
Promises**. Keep existing promises and reduce the unsus-
tainable burden on the Social Security and Medicare Systems, by enabling every American to accumulate sufficient wealth-producing assets to provide each person with
an adequate and secure taxable income from property,
independent of Social Security and Medicare benefits and
incomes from other sources. Based on conservative projec-
tions of U.S. growth potential, by age 65 a child born today could accumulate a capital estate of nearly $500,000,
generating $1.6 million in after-tax dividends over that
period.

**Restructure the Credit and Tax Systems to
Encourage Universal Health Care through the
Private Sector**. Capital Homestead reforms,
supplemented by health care vouchers for the poor, would
provide a sustainable way to finance the health care
system. These reforms would empower each citizen and
family with the means to enjoy and pay for affordable,
quality health coverage of their choice. Through market-
disciplined, comprehensive health care enterprises that
are owned and controlled by health care providers and
health care subscribers (patients), the doctor-patient
relationship could be restored, while providing greater
insurance portability, accountability and lower
administrative overhead costs throughout the system.

**Solve the Home Foreclosure Crisis and Make
Home Ownership Accessible to all Citizens**. Starting
in communities with homes whose market values are de-
flated due to the sub-prime mortgage crisis, resident-
owned Homeowners Equity Corporations (HECs) could
receive interest-free credit to buy up the foreclosed properties. As occupants of the homes in default pay the HEC
their monthly rents (which could be supplemented with

housing vouchers for the poor), these would be applied toward debt service, using pre-tax dollars to pay off the loans that the HEC used to purchase the foreclosed properties. As they make their regular monthly lease payments, these renters would become full owners of HEC shares and their dwellings.

Stop Federal Reserve Monetization of Government Debt. Terminate use of the Federal Reserve's powers to create debt-backed money, to support foreign currencies, or to buy and sell primary or secondary Treasury securities. This would reduce excessive government spending and improve accountability. It would force government to borrow for deficits directly from savers in the open market.

Stabilize the Value of the Currency. Require the Federal Reserve to create a stable, asset-backed currency to encourage ownership by all citizens of productive private sector assets rather than non-productive public sector debt or future ownership monopolies.

Reduce Dependency on Existing Accumulations of Savings for Financing Growth. Require the Federal Reserve to distinguish between "sound" and "unsound" uses of credit, by providing interest-free money to expand bank credit to enable every American to become an owner of a viable accumulation of new income-producing assets. This would reduce America's dependency on existing accumulations of savings, corporate retained earnings, or foreign government wealth funds advantaged by America's growing trade imbalances.

Restore the Federal Reserve to Its Original Function. Require the Federal Reserve System to supply sufficient money and credit through local commercial banks to meet the liquidity and broadened ownership needs of an expanding market-disciplined economy. Such "Federal Reserve-monetized" loans would be subject to appropriate feasibility standards administered by the banks and limited only by the goal of maintaining a stable value for the dollar. Unsound or usurious uses of credit, such as the speculative credit that created sub-prime home mortgages and the global financial meltdown and the growing burden of consumer and government debt, would be financed from the accumulations of the wealthy that can afford the risks.

Democratize Ownership of the Federal Reserve. Provide every citizen a single, lifetime, non-transferable voting share in the nation's central bank — the network of twelve regional Federal Reserve banks. This would ensure that the Federal Reserve's board of governors is broadly representative of all groups affected by Federal Reserve policy, and that power over future money creation is spread widely among all citizens.

Discourage Monopolies and Monopolistic Ownership. Link all economic reforms to methods that discourage privileged access to monopolistic accumulations of private property ownership of the means of production. Enforce anti-trust laws by providing access to interest-free capital credit to encourage broadly owned new competitors to enhance and sustain market-oriented growth.

Introduce a Market-Driven Wage and Price System. Gradually eliminate rigid, artificially protected wage and price levels and other restrictions on free trade that afford special privileges to some industries, businesses and workers at the expense of American and foreign customers of U.S. products. Replace subsidies with interest-free credit incentives to farmers who wish to associate voluntarily in cooperatives and in enterprises jointly owned by farmers and workers, including integrated agri-businesses. The income generated by farmer-owned enterprises would supplement farm incomes and reduce the need for subsidies.

Restore Property Rights in Corporate Equity. Restore the original rights of "private property" to all owners of corporate equity, particularly with respect to the right to profits and in the sharing of control over corporate policies. Preserve traditional powers of professional managers held accountable by Justice-Based Management corporate governance structures.

Offer a More Just Social Contract for Workers. A top priority during the next decade would be developing a more just "social contract" for persons employed in the private sector. This would be geared toward establishing maximum ownership incentives. Instead of inflationary "wage system" increases, employees would begin to earn future increases in income through production bonuses, equity accumulations, and profit earnings. These "bottom-line" rewards would be linked to workers' individual contributions, and to the productivity and success of their work team and the enterprise for which they work.

Encourage More Harmonious Worker, Management Relations. Promote the right of non-management workers to form democratic unions and other voluntary associations. Instead of promoting the traditional "conflict model" of industrial relations, however, "labor" unions would be encouraged to transform themselves into democratic "ownership unions." These ownership unions could become society's primary institutions for promoting a free market version of economic justice, while continuing to negotiate and advance workers' economic interests, including worker ownership rights and Justice-Based Management policies.

Under Capital Homesteading, unions could expand their role in a free market system by educating and expanding their membership to include all citizen-shareholders. Ownership unions would enhance the property rights of all shareholders by enhancing management accountability and transparency, and protecting against unjust executive compensation schemes.

Promote a Life-Enhancing Physical and Cultural Environment. Encourage special ownership incentives for those engaged in research and development, especially in the search for new and sustainable sources of energy, ecological restoration and labor-saving technologies. Provide sufficient low-cost credit and royalty-free licensing for enterprises capable of commercializing life-enhancing technologies developed for the military and space programs. Subsidize the development of new methods of conserving and recycling non-replenishable and limited natural resources that are vital to civilization's long-term survival, at least until suitable substitutes can be discovered and developed. Promote the teaching at all levels of education of universal principles of personal morality and social morality that are based on the inherent dignity and sovereignty of every human person within all institutions of a just social order, including the State.

Reduce Public Sector Costs. Provide America's military, policemen and firemen, teachers, and other public-sector workers with a growing and more direct equity stake in the free enterprise system, both as a supplement to their costly pension plans and so that they will better understand and defend the institution of private property. Whenever feasible, transform government-owned enterprises and services into competitive private sector companies, by offering their workers (and customers and other stakeholders in capital-intensive operations like TVA) opportunities to participate in ownership, governance and profits.

Establish Workable Demonstrations of Capital Homesteading at the Community, State, Regional and Global Levels. Launch several Capital Homesteading demonstrations. These would be most effective in areas of high unemployment. A major objective would be to evaluate ownership-broadening Federal Reserve reforms, innovative broadened ownership mechanisms, advanced concepts of worker participation in decision-making, and servant leadership developments like Justice-Based Management.

Encourage State and local governments and other countries to promote widespread capital ownership as a basic "Just Third Way" framework for building a sound market economy.

Study the feasibility of a national and global citizen-owned "Land and Natural Resources Bank" to plan development of Nature's resources, receive rentals for use of land and natural resources, and distribute citizen dividends among the population. With the leadership of the United States, urge the United Nations and other international agencies to encourage the use of such economic development vehicles in order to bring about "peace through justice" in conflict-torn countries.

Initiate New Challenges for Multinationals. Provide special encouragement to U.S.-based multinational corporations and global financial institutions to become instruments of peace and a more just world economic order, by broadening access to their ownership base to all citizens of the world community. Encourage businesses to open up future ownership opportunities as they begin harnessing the resources of the sea, the airways and other planets.

Promote a New Global Monetary System based on full production and full participation in production instead of inflation and debt. Encourage the convening of a second "Bretton Woods Conference" to consider the implications of the Kelsonian binary economic model on global currency standards, the feasibility of a single global currency, and more just foreign exchange rates. The new policy should seek to reform global financial markets to address the challenge of global poverty and sustainable development, as well as leveling the playing field among nations for global free and open trade.

These measures, of course, are expressed in necessarily broad terms, but they give a good idea of the approach of the Just Third Way as applied in Capital Homesteading. The orientation is removal of barriers to full participation in the common good so that every person has an equal opportunity to acquire and develop virtue and so become as fully human as possible.

3. The First Pillar

The first pillar of an economically just society is that, in the Just Third Way, the State should only exercise an extremely limited role in the economy. Being made by people for people, although consistent with human nature and ordinarily necessary for our full development as persons, the State is nevertheless only a tool. It is a highly specialized and extremely powerful tool, but still only a tool. When the State no longer serves the purpose for which it is designed and intended, it must be reoriented and repaired so that it once again functions properly.

With respect to economics, the proper role of the State is to ensure as far as possible that all citizens have the same opportunity to participate in wealth creation on an equal basis with everyone else. Generally construed as providing "a level playing field," the State's job typically consists of establishing and maintaining a strong juridical order consistent with the natural moral law (the "rule of law"), setting standards for weights and measures — including the currency — policing abuses, and enforcing agreements when parties to a contract have a dispute or disagreement concerning the "meeting of the minds."

The State's task is not to initiate, create, or control persons, institutions, relationships, or anything else. It does, however, have a limited role in clarifying and promulgating definitions of institutions and specifying how rights are to be exercised. This is usually by the State putting its "imprimatur" on what "public opinion" (A. V. Dicey's term) has already decided. Never, however, does this extend to the State having the sort of absolute power that claims the ability to change definitions, develop new definitions, or in any way (in Keynes's words) "re-edit" the dictionary. State absolutism is the basis for Keynes's claim, in his *Treatise on Money* (1930), developed out of the tenets of the British Currency School, that the State alone has the power to decide of what "money" consists, who may contract and for what, and who may participate in the common good. Followed logically, Keynes's understanding of money abolishes private property and liberty (freedom of association/contract), the two most important props for the maintenance and protection of the right to life.

Even the corporation, specifically a "creature of law" is not, in social justice, created by the State, but by private citizens organizing, and obtaining official sanction and protection of their acts as a corporate body. The State is supposed to regulate transactions and relationships that stray too far from acceptable norms established by consensus, and, as far as possible, bring matters back into conformity with human nature when failure to conform to these standards has a materially harmful effect on individuals, groups, or the common good as a whole. The State does not have the power to create anything, especially money, a claim that (as we noted) effectively abolishes private property and freedom of association.

Further, as a human creation itself, the State is compelled to act in the best interests of its citizens, even those instances in which a majority wishes to override or abolish the rights of a minority, or a minority seeks to use its political or economic power to oppress the majority . . . even or especially if the minority believes it to be for the majority's own good. While there is a wide area in which the majority or minority should rule, and may do so in fact, there is a line that must not be crossed. That line is crossed whenever those in power seek to use the State's monopoly over the instruments of coercion for its own advantage, and in contravention of the natural moral law to abolish or inhibit the free exercise of natural rights in ways not demanded by the common good or the individual good of persons and groups.

The State's job is to promote the *general* welfare, not the *particular* welfare of any individual or group to the disadvantage of others, no matter how large or important the group presumably being benefited. One of the premises of capitalism is that the State can safely ignore its responsibility for the general welfare by taking a *laissez faire* approach to particular welfare. Socialism, on the other hand, assumes that the general welfare is best promoted by having the State take care of each individual's particular welfare. Both socialism and capitalism assume that the general welfare is the sum of society's particular welfares, and that what best promotes particular welfare automatically secures the general welfare.

Both capitalism and socialism thereby manage to be wrong in the same way, and so, while seemingly diametrically opposed, always end up as virtual mirror images of each other. Both, by one route or another, end up at the Servile State, with an indistinguishable private or State elite in charge, and the great mass of people in a condition of utter dependency on that elite. Thus, both capitalism and socialism, whatever we might call them or try to argue otherwise, offend against essential human dignity at the most basic level. Both capitalism and socialism are "top down" and fail to respect people as people. Both capitalism and socialism attempt to impose their respective (if indistinguishable) visions of what is good by force, and maintain those visions through coercion.

In contrast, the Just Third Way approaches matters from the "bottom" up. The underlying problem in the difference between capitalism and socialism, and the Just Third Way lies in our understanding of the common good, a more precise and meaningful term than general welfare. (The reasons the American Founding Fathers used "general welfare" instead of "common good," and "pursuit of happiness" instead of "acquiring and developing virtue," while important, would be a diversion, and are peripheral to our main point. These issues will not be covered in this discussion.)

The common good is not a vague concept, nor is it automatic collectivism. Instead, the common good is something that can be defined with scientific precision and in a manner consistent with essential human nature. The common good is not the collection of particular goods of individual persons or groups. Instead, the common good is the network of institutions within the overall framework of the social order — and, in fact, that largely make up the social order — within which humanity as "political animals" acquires and develops virtue, thereby becoming more fully human. The specific job of this institutional network is to assist individuals to acquire and develop virtue: "pursue happiness." By this means individual human beings realize their human potential to the optimum degree possible without harm to other individuals, groups, or the common good as a whole.

When our institutions are flawed to such a degree that they either do not assist us in pursuing happiness, or actively and materially inhibit us in the task of realizing our fullest human potential, it becomes our individual responsibility to organize with like-minded others and work to reform our institutions. Our goal is twofold: 1) restructure our institutions so that they once again assist us in our pursuit of happiness, and 2) ensure that our understanding of happiness conforms to universal standards of virtue.

The means by which we reform our institutional environment to conform it to the Just Third Way is the "act of social justice." This was ably summarized by William J. Ferree, S.M., Ph.D., described by one European philosopher as "America's greatest social philosopher,"[1] in his short work, *Introduction to Social Justice*.[2] Briefly, it is clear that individuals are frequently helpless when faced with unjust social structures and problems that afflict the whole of society. Faced with the impossible task of trying to change things individually, the rational person will not destroy him- or herself in a hopeless struggle, however gallant and virtuous it might seem, but will give up, and go along to get along. No one, after all, is required to do the impossible.

---

[1] Rev. Andrew F. Morlion, O.P., Ph.D., *United Peoples*, No. 14.
[2] New York: Paulist Press, 1948.

As Ferree demonstrated, however, the individual is far from helpless — but only when he or she organizes with others, and carries out directed acts of social virtue. This cannot be done as individuals, but as members of a group in an organized and coherent program of specific reform. Ferree identified certain "laws and characteristics" of social justice by means of which we are empowered to act directly on the institutions of the common good.

The first "law" of social justice is that the common good must be kept inviolate. That is, "in all private dealings, in all exercise of individual justice, the Common Good must be a primary object of solicitude. To attack or to endanger the Common Good in order to attain some private end, no matter how good or how necessary this latter may be in its own order, is social injustice and is wrong."[3] If what we propose to do violates anyone else's rights, or harms the common good in any material fashion (*e.g.*, abolishing the institution of private property, or redefining another individual or group as "non-persons"), we cannot justify that act.

The second "law" of social justice is "cooperation not conflict." Socialism and capitalism both understand the common good as a collection of particular, that is, individual goods. When we confuse individual goods and the common good — or, worse, common *goods* and the common *good* — we necessarily put all individual goods and common goods in conflict with one another. Instead of trying to establish the ascendancy of our particular good or goods over those of others, or one or two common goods over the totality of goods held in trust by the State for the benefit of society, we have to realize two things.

One, the common good is not a collection of individual goods, or even those common goods that, for the sake of expedience, the State "owns." Two, realization of our individual goods, and the optimal enjoyment of common goods, can only take place within a strong juridical

---

[3] *Introduction to Social Justice*. Washington, DC: Center for Economic and Social Justice, 1997, 35.

framework in conformity with the natural law and to which all citizens have given their consent, whether explicit or tacit. This requires that people and groups cooperate within the institutional environment of the common good in order to gain the optimal benefit without harming the rights or interests of others.

The third "law" of social justice is that "one's first particular good is one's own place in the common good." This law is a logical extension of the first two laws. The first law is that we cannot hijack any part of the common good, that is, any institution (such as an individual right to choose or private property), or the common good as a whole to advance our individual interest(s). This third law is that we cannot hijack any part of the common good or the common good as a whole to advance our *institutional* interest(s), that is, our group or groups over other groups or the common good as a whole. Groups must cooperate, not come into conflict, within the institutional framework of the common good in the same way as individuals.

The fourth "law" of social justice is that "everyone is directly and personally responsible for the common good." This is because the common good is made up of institutions. These institutions are, in turn, made up of sub-institutions, and these sub-institutions are made up of sub-sub-institutions, and so on, *ad infinitum*, down, or, more accurately if less usual, *up*, to the individual. "Up" is more correct because all institutions are made to serve humanity, not the other way around; the "organizational chart" for society should be an inverted pyramid or diamond. This has the State at the bottom, supporting, empowering, and enriching others.

Further, these institutions combine with other institutions at their "level" of the common good to form milieux, or the various media of life within particular contexts. As we might expect, these milieux are made up of sub-milieux, and these sub-milieux of sub-sub-milieux, and so on, "up" to all individuals in society, on whose natural rights the whole towering and complex superstructure of the common good ultimately rests. These relationships are in a constant state of flux, to such a degree that the social order can be described as being "radically unstable," at least in the sense that changing between milieux, moving among institutions, interacting with other groups and individuals, and so on, means that each person's specific social situation and the relationships of society are never the same. Thus, because everything ultimately derives from the individual and the social rights possessed absolutely by each and every human person, it necessarily follows that each and every human person has a direct and individual responsibility for the common good.

The fifth "law" of social justice is that "higher institutions must never displace lower ones." This is the principle of subsidiarity. That is, because each and every individual has a personal responsibility for the common good at his or her level, institutions at "higher" — or "lower" — levels of the common must never take over the functions of institutions at other levels. They would otherwise be usurping the responsibility and thus power of those who subsist at that level. Regardless of whatever level of the common good we're talking about, "insiders" are the ones primarily responsible for their own institutions. "Outsiders" can assist, and even in an emergency take over from the insiders temporarily, but never displace the institution itself. That would be to impose a condition of dependency on those who subsist within that institution, which is directly contrary to the demands of human dignity, and thus of social justice.

The sixth "law" of social justice is "freedom of association." This is the "liberty" of which America's Founding Fathers spoke. It does not mean license, that is, doing whatever you want, when you want. There is some of that, but only within the strong juridical framework of the common good, and only if doing what you want when you want does not harm anybody or anything, including yourself. The reason freedom of association is a law of social justice is that the act of social justice is necessarily *social*, and therefore social justice is only possible if people are free to associate.

The seventh "law" of social justice is that "all vital interests should be organized." As Aristotle observed, "man is by nature a political animal."[4] That being the case, humanity acts in accordance with its own nature when it acts politically, that is, in an organized and structured manner within the *polis*, that is, the political unit.

In addition to the laws of social justice, we also have six essential characteristics of social justice. Comparing these characteristics with our proposed action, we can make a good determination whether what we are engaged in is truly "social justice," and not just extended individualism or collectivism.

The first characteristic of social justice is that individuals as individuals cannot carry out acts of social justice. The act of social justice is something that can only be carried out by members of groups, that is, as a political act.

The second characteristic of social justice is that it takes time. This makes sense if we stop to think about it. "Virtue" is defined as "the habit of doing good." Building good individual habits can take a lifetime. How much more time, then, can it take to overcome social inertia and build good *institutional* habits? Of course, this does not mean that it is not possible to change institutional habits overnight, but do not count on it as a general thing.

The third characteristic of social justice is that nothing is impossible. As we've already noted, individuals frequently feel helpless in the face of what seem to be (and frequently are) insurmountable social problems — speaking individually. The common good, however, is composed of an effectively infinite number of institutions, every single one of which was made by human beings. The necessity for these institutions is "hard wired" into our nature, but the specific form that the institutions take is due to conscious decisions made at some point by human beings. Human beings made our institutions, and human beings

---

[4] *The Politics*, I.ii.

can therefore remake our institutions — once we approach the task with the tools that social justice gives us.

The fourth characteristic of social justice is constant vigilance. As we can see from the structure of the common good, the social order is in a constant and bewildering state of flux. We have different levels of institutions, institutions combining and recombining to form different milieux, and the people, groups, and sub-groups within institutions and milieux are constantly changing the relationships between all these elements. That being the case, we must keep a constant watch on our institutional environment — the common good — to make certain that it continues to meet our needs and wants adequately. It will, of course, never do so perfectly. Should, however, our institutions stray *too* far from their assigned roles, we must organize with others to correct the situation and put things back on course.

The fifth characteristic of social justice is effectiveness. We can have all the good will in the world, but if what we propose to do in order to improve the general welfare or ameliorate the condition of the poor or anyone else will not work, we would be acting in a socially useless or wasteful manner. It is not enough to intend to do the right thing. The intended good must stand a reasonable chance of being accomplished. Further, the good must be accomplished without any unintended but anticipated non-objectively evil consequences. That is, we must not only *be* right, we must *do* right. This transcends expedients allowed by the "principle of double effect." A virtuous and glorious defeat just to make a point, or to prove how much better we are than others is not a socially just option.

The sixth characteristic of social justice is that organizing with others to restructure our institutional environment for the better is not optional. It is, on the contrary, a rigid obligation imposed on us by our very nature. As political animals, human beings ordinarily are expected to acquire and develop virtue (pursue happiness) within a well-structured social order. That being the case, when the social order is flawed we owe it to ourselves as members of the human race to organize with others to get things back on track when necessary.

The bottom line is that the State has a definite role to play, but the State's role is not as sweeping as the socialists claim, nor as the capitalists eventually (and inevitably) demand. Instead, as should be obvious from the above discussion on the laws and characteristics of social justice, *lex ratio*, "rule of law" — reason — necessarily takes precedence over the capitalists' and the socialists' *lex voluntas*, "rule of whim" — will. The State does not determine what is right or wrong. Consequently the State cannot either impose desired results, or stand aside and let people do what they will, whether or not what they will is in conformity with nature. As A. V. Dicey pointed out, the State, no less than every individual in the State, is subject to the law. Neither the State nor anyone else can "'re-edit' the dictionary."

4. The Second Pillar

A basic tenet of the Just Third Way is that the free market is the best means for determining just wages, just profits, and just prices. The free market is in many respects a natural extension of, and a complement to the rights of private property, the free enjoyment of which is a necessary corollary to ownership itself. As William Cobbett, the "Apostle of Distributism" explained,

> Freedom is not an empty sound; it is not an abstract idea; it is not a thing that nobody can feel. It means, — and it means nothing else, — the full and quiet enjoyment of your own property. If you have not this, if this be not well secured to you, you may call yourself what you will, but you are a slave.[1]

(Distributism is the somewhat misleading term for the system of widespread direct ownership of the means of production that Belloc and his confrere, G. K. Chesterton, advocated.) Thus, the free market is simply the power in aggregate of people doing what they will with what they own, constrained by the bounds of common sense and justice. In the ordinary course of events, the free market is a concrete, and possibly the most important daily manifestation of human liberty. Another term for liberty is the natural right of free association, a fundamental law of social justice and thus one of the foundation stones of human dignity.

From what we read in the previous chapter in this book regarding the laws and characteristics of social justice, it should be glaringly obvious that "free association," especially in the marketplace, does not mean *laissez faire*, or doing whatever you want when you want to do it with no restraint from any quarter, regardless of the conse-

---

[1] *A History of the Protestant Reformation in England and Ireland*, 1827, §456.

quences. Very much the contrary — liberty implies action
within a just social order. This in turn implies a strong
juridical order to maintain that social order within tolerable limits. As the great German jurist Heinrich Rommen
explained,

> The foundation of law is justice. "Truth grants or re-
> fuses the highest crown to the products of positive leg-
> islation, and they draw from truth their true moral
> force" (Franz Brentano). But truth is conformity with
> reality. And just as the real and the true are one, so
> too the true and the just are ultimately one. *Veritas
> facit legem* ["truth makes law"]. And in this profound
> sense of the unity of truth and justice the words, "And
> the truth shall make you free," are applicable to the
> community of men under law. True freedom consists
> in being bound by justice.[2]

Understood in this way, the free market is the antithe-
sis of capitalism as well as socialism. Under both capitalism and socialism, significant barriers are raised against
ordinary people becoming owners of the means of production. In socialism these barriers are legal, and private
property is abolished outright. In capitalism, institutional
barriers and even implicit assumptions about money and
credit — the most common means of acquiring and possessing private property — (most of which assumptions
are distorted or just plain wrong) erect barriers that prevent the great majority of people from becoming owners.

The first — and last — thing always to remember about
money is that, to be legitimate and serve the purpose for
which it is intended, "money" must always — *always* —
be *directly* backed by a private property interest in the
present value of existing inventories of wealth (marketable goods and services) or the present value of an anticipated future stream of income generated by the production (and sale) of marketable goods and services. Money is
directly backed by the present value of existing or future

---

[2] Heinrich Rommen, *The Natural Law*. Indianapolis, Indiana:
Liberty Fund, Inc., 1998, 236-237.

production only through the link provided by the institution of private property.

An indirect link between money and production, or (worse) no link at all, is a form of theft — a violation of private property — on the part of whoever issues the currency or creates the money. This may be one reason why the framers of the U.S. Constitution specifically removed the power of Congress to "emit bills of credit" — issue contracts that can be accepted as money — from the first draft of the Constitution . . . over the protests of some Convention delegates who feared that this might unnecessarily limit the powers of Congress in a national emergency. To be legitimate and fill its proper role, money is necessarily linked to production of marketable goods and services. In modern terms, "money" is a derivative of production, and is a fraud (a "fictitious bill") unless the issuer of the money has a direct private property stake in the production that backs the money.

The end result in either capitalism or socialism, however, is the same: the establishment of the Servile State. The great mass of people becomes economically dependent on a private or State elite that illegitimately takes over private property by controlling money and credit. The elite does this by preventing people from becoming productive, or by controlling the means and the manner in which people can produce. Whether the State elite controls the private elite that controls the means of production (as in socialism), or whether the private elite that controls the means of production controls the State elite (as in capitalism), becomes a matter of complete indifference to anyone who subsists on wages or welfare alone. The only things that matter is that the income keeps coming, and that the spirit of liberty is sufficiently quelled in the human heart.

The problem in a technologically advanced economy such as the world now for the most part enjoys, is that the system will eventually break down unless the great mass of people become direct owners of the means of production. When the production of most marketable goods and services is due not to human labor, but to machinery, a well-ordered system absolutely requires that people have access to the means of acquiring and possessing private property in the non-human means of production, as formerly they enjoyed natural access to the direct ownership of their own labor.

Of course, everyone is aware that in the past, when human labor was the primary means of production, there were always attempts to prevent people from enjoying the full fruits of their natural ownership of labor, just as today there are continuing efforts to keep people from becoming owners of technology. Preventing people from enjoying the fruits of ownership of their own labor is called "slavery." Preventing people from becoming owners of the non-human factors of production and forcing them to rely on wages alone is called "wage slavery," or "the wage system."

Not that there is much difference in the justifications used for the two systems. For example, as David Christy explained in his appalling rationalization of chattel slavery published on the eve of the American Civil War, *Cotton is King* (1855), the economic health of Anglo-American civilization, that is, the British Empire and the United States, was presumed to rely absolutely on the slave cultivation of cotton and other agricultural products needed to supply the mills of Manchester and the factories of the northeastern United States. By no other means could the wealth and power of Anglo-American civilization be preserved — or so Christy took as his basic premise.

Further, Christy claimed that black slaves were fitted by nature to fill no other role, living in utter barbarism in their home continent until brought to America as slaves and raised as far as their nature permitted. The observed behavior of free blacks presumably proved them incapable of the sustained effort necessary to succeed in being productive because they could not be forced to work. Whites were not physically suited to the cultivation of cotton, coming from the temperate climate of Europe. Blacks, Christy contended, were especially designed by nature to be guided by whites and put to work in a climate that most closely matched that of their native land.

And so on — all argued with sincerity and supported by a great mass of statistical data. The presentation was very effective in convincing a great many people, then and now, of the truth of the assertions. The logical flaws in Christy's argument are obvious to anyone familiar with the Aristotelian/Thomist basis of binary economics. These flaws, however, remain hidden to those who take as a given the same assumptions as Christy about human nature as well as money and credit that afflict us today. Christy's argument was persuasive enough to provide a presumably sound economic argument for secession of the southern states when they feared that abolition of slavery would be mandated with the election of Abraham Lincoln. *Cotton is King* was quoted at length in Congress and in the press in debates about slavery.

Tellingly, the arguments in favor of chattel slavery do not differ substantially from the arguments advanced in favor of the concentrated ownership of capital that characterizes industrial capitalism and socialism. The main difference is in the factor of production being monopolized. In the chattel slavery system, ownership of human labor is separated from the slave and vested in a master. In capitalism, ownership of technology is separated from the worker and vested in the capitalist. In socialism, ownership of both technology and labor is separated from natural persons and vested in the State.

Just as David Christy provided the economic argument to support chattel slavery, John Maynard Keynes provided (or at least congealed into an unquestioned dogma) the economic argument to support the Servile State of capitalism and socialism, that is, wage and welfare slavery. These arguments are well known to anyone who has ever read the book that made Keynes's reputation, *The Economic Consequences of the Peace* (1919), or the Keynesian "bible," *The General Theory of Employment, Interest, and Money* (1936). The most important Keynesian dogma, established solidly on the wrong definition of money, is found in *The Economic Consequences of the Peace*, and calls forcibly to mind a similar claim by David Christy with respect to slavery:

> The immense accumulations of fixed capital which, to the great benefit of mankind, were built up during the half century before the war, could never have come about in a Society where wealth was divided equitably.[3]

Examined objectively of course, the reasons given why a presumably economically healthy society requires chattel slavery, capitalism, or socialism all have one thing in common. They all share the same assumption that ownership of capital *must* be concentrated if the economic health of society is to be maintained. And why must ownership of the means of production be concentrated rather than "divided equitably"? Because capital formation can, presumably, only be financed out of existing accumulations of savings, and only the rich (and the richer, the better, to maximize economic and social progress) have the ability to cut consumption and save. Ownership of the means of production must be concentrated and private property in the means of production effectively abolished in order to justify limited redistribution of the fruits of ownership to non-owners.

Everything in Keynesian economics flows from this assumption. To understand this, we need only realize that this Keynesian dogma is, broken down to its essential elements, the belief that 1) Capital formation *cannot* be financed except out of existing accumulations of savings. 2) "Saving" consists *exclusively* of cutting consumption. 3) "Money" is *solely* determined and created by the State, and 4) No economic activity can be carried out except that which is directly sanctioned by the State.[4]

Capitalism (and, more obviously, socialism and slavery) is therefore as far from being a "free market" as it is pos-

---

[3] *The Economic Consequences of the Peace*, Chapter 2, Section III.

[4] See Thomas Hobbes, *Leviathan*, II.22.

sible to get and still delude yourself that capitalism and the free market are the same thing. The main difference between capitalism and socialism with respect to the free market is that, where capitalism claims that a free market is good (at least for a few), perhaps even the greatest thing that exists, its adherents recognize that a few socialist expedients may be necessary to keep people quiet. For its part, socialism claims the free market is evil, although a few capitalist expedients may be necessary (to be enjoyed, of course, only by a few) to keep the economy running.

Once capitalism and socialism meet on the common ground of the Servile State, however, we readily understand why, 1) a free market is so essential to basic human dignity, and 2) equating capitalism and the free market, or claiming that "free market reforms" make socialism less unjust is simply a way of fooling ourselves.

The fact is that the free market, circumscribed within a strict juridical order and functioning in reasonable compliance with the natural moral law, especially with respect to the natural rights of free association (liberty) and private property, is the best and most efficient way to secure economic choice. The free choices of both producers and consumers, each offering his or her subjective opinion as to the value of goods and services being exchanged (with neither under any compulsion to buy or sell), is the best way to determine the just market price for each input to the productive process. In such a free and open marketplace, both freedom and efficiency are maximized — a point on which we can agree with Milton Friedman.[5]

Then there is the fact that adherence to such unthinking dogma simply obscures the real problem with the free market — which is that the so-called free market is anything but free when the great mass of people lack access to the means of acquiring and possessing private property

---

[5] Milton Friedman, *Capitalism and Freedom*. Chicago, Illinois: University of Chicago Press, 1982.

in the means of production. Until and unless that criterion is met, no economy can be called truly free.

Ownership of at least a moderate stake of income-generating assets is essential not only as the chief support of individual human dignity and a democratic political order, but to equalize the condition and bargaining position of participants in the marketplace. Alexis de Tocqueville made this strikingly clear in his monumental sociological study of the United States during the Jacksonian era, *Democracy in America* (1835, 1840). As de Tocqueville related in a passage of which most people fail to realize the significance,

> In democratic countries as well as elsewhere most of the branches of productive industry are carried on at a small cost by men little removed by their wealth or education above the level those whom they employ. These manufacturing speculators are extremely numerous; their interests differ; they cannot therefore easily concert or combine their exertions. On the other hand, the workmen have always some sure resources which enable them to refuse to work when they cannot get what they conceive to be the fair price of their labor. In the constant struggle for wages that is going on between these two classes, their strength is divided and success alternates from one to the other.

> It is even probable that in the end the interest of the working class will prevail, for the high wages which they have already obtained make them every day less dependent on their masters, and as they grow more independent, they have greater facilities for obtaining a further increase of wages.

> I shall take for example that branch of productive industry which is still at the present day the most generally followed in France and in almost all the countries of the world, the cultivation of the soil. In France most of those who labor for hire in agriculture are themselves owners of certain plots of ground, which just enable them to subsist without working for anyone else. When these laborers come to offer their serv-

ices to a neighboring landowner or farmer, if he re-
fuses them a certain rate of wages they retire to their
own small property and await another opportunity.[6]

Arguing an unsuspected familiarity with de Tocqueville's work, in this passage we can discern concepts
that Pope Pius XI seems to have lifted wholesale and inserted into *Quadragesimo Anno* ("On the Restructuring of
the Social Order"), 1931, notably paragraphs 59-63. More
to the point, however, we find affirmation of Belloc's (and
Cobbett's) principle that the Servile State consists not in
the formal institution of slavery, but in the powerlessness
and consequent dependent status that afflicts those who
do not own an adequate capital stake.

The Servile State consists principally of removing the
free choice whether or not to work by making subsistence
completely dependent on wage or welfare income. Clearly,
then (just as Cobbett claimed) true slavery consists of the
inability to enjoy the fruits of ownership of the means of
production, whether labor or capital. In contrast, the free
market consists of a marketplace in which everyone not
only has the *right* to participate freely as consumers and
producers, by means of both their labor and their capital,
but also has the means to *exercise* that right in a meaningful fashion, that is, *freely*.

---

[6] "Influence of Democracy on Wages," *Democracy in America*,
Volume II.

5. The Third Pillar

In the previous chapter, we discovered that it is not sufficient to call something a free market, and yet ignore everything that makes a market free. The institution that alone has the potential to make or keep a market free is widespread direct ownership of capital. From this it follows logically that, even if everyone has a legal right to be an owner, that right is meaningless unless 1) someone actually *is* an owner, and 2) that ownership is *real* ownership. This chapter covers what we mean by "ownership," that is, the rights of private property.

Our task, therefore, is to define what we mean by "property." We already know that this thing we call property is somehow important, but that realization does not do us much good until and unless we know of what this important thing called property consists.

First, most people assume that when you say "property," you are referring to what someone owns. That is close — but not close enough. Rather, property is the natural right every human being has to be an owner, and the socially determined bundle of rights that define how an owner may use that which he or she possesses. That is, property is the right to and the rights over a thing that is owned in relationship to all others; "property" is not the thing itself.

Unfortunately, for many people in the world today, this is a meaningless distinction. With the exception of their labor, which is declining in value relative to technology as technology becomes increasingly productive, most people do not have private property in anything that could be considered productive. Those people that do possess a few equity shares representing a nominal minority ownership interest in a business enterprise frequently do not enjoy the full bundle of rights that historically in America and under the common law of England accompany ownership.

While the opportunity to become an owner of the means of production is generally considered a hallmark of "free market capitalism" in the United States, that opportunity (as we have already seen) is as meaningless as the oxymoronic equation of the free market with capitalism. Adding insult to injury, unless a shareholder has a controlling interest in a company, the courts have decided that the only effective right that the shareholder can exercise is to sell the asset. The most important rights of private property — the rights to enjoy the income generated by and to control the disposition of what is owned — are completely subject to the whim of whoever has a controlling interest.

Ironically, the stripping of rights from minority owners — a direct, full frontal assault on the institution of private property — is due in large measure to the actions by one of the "high priests of capitalism": Henry Ford. Frankly, capitalism is only marginally palatable because, however distorted, it is based on the natural right to private property and the correlative rights of private property. By effectively taking away the principal rights of private property — the right to enjoy the income generated by and otherwise exercise control over what is owned — Henry Ford sabotaged the very system he is credited with helping to establish and maintain. How this came about is a story that is almost epic in scope.

In the first quarter of the 20th century, Henry Ford decided to finance a plant expansion using retained earnings instead of selling new equity or borrowing the money. The Dodge brothers, minority owners, protested. They wanted the dividends to which they were entitled under the traditional rights of private property. Ford refused to pay dividends. The Dodge brothers sued.

In *Dodge v. Ford Motor Company*,[1] among other issues, the court redefined the traditional right to receive the

---

[1] 204 Mich. 459, 170 N.W. 668. (Mich. 1919).

"fruits of ownership" (*i.e.*, income from what is owned —
dividends) for minority shareholders as limited to the
power to sell their shares if they were not happy with the
dividend policy of the majority owner(s).

The court ruled, in effect, that minority shareholders
are able to enjoy their full "fruits of ownership," including
the right to receive any and all income generated by what
is owned, only if the majority owner so agrees. That is, the
majority owner(s) alone, through control of the Board of
Directors, have the right to set dividend policy for a company, and do not need the consent of a minority owner or
owner(s) to withhold that which belongs by right to the
minority owner(s).

Henry Ford built his case on the "business judgment
rule." That is, if the individual elected by the shareholders
(who happened to be Henry Ford, as he retained the majority block of shares) decided it was in the best interests
of the company — and therefore of the shareholders — to
stop or reduce payment of dividends, the minority shareholders had no recourse other than to retain their shares
and take whatever the majority owner(s) chose to dish out
— unless they could prove that the company did not need
the profits for the business. The alternative was to exercise their "take-it-or-leave-it" right to sell their shares and
wash their hands of the whole business — in other words,
to exercise their property rights solely to become non-
owners. As proving a negative (that the company does not
need the profits for business purposes) is logically impossible, the court effectively gave absolute power to the
board of directors, ignoring the rights of minority owners.

What is also frequently ignored in analyses of the case
is the fact that Henry Ford had dismissed another right of
private property, that of control. He had previously
blocked every effort of the minority shareholders to have
input into decisions and exercise some degree of control
over the business, such as design improvements and mar-
keting strategy. This was particularly egregious with respect to the Dodge brothers, who owned the next largest

block of shares (10%) after Henry Ford, and who were increasingly unhappy with Ford's dictatorial actions.

Consequently, prior to their lawsuit over Ford's restriction of dividend payments, the Dodge brothers began setting up their own automobile manufacturing company in secret, using their Ford dividends to finance the effort. Ford got wind of this and began withholding dividends. Ford was also suspected of wanting to reduce the price of Ford automobiles as a way of justifying the proposed reduction in dividend payouts and reducing the company value per share.

After the Michigan Supreme Court ruled in his favor, Ford threatened to set up another rival automobile manufacturing company, probably to be wholly owned by Ford personally. This was apparently as a way to compel the Dodge brothers to sell their shares back to the Ford Motor Company at the reduced value per share that Ford had manipulated. In this he was successful — and thereby undermined another right of private property, that of disposal, by taking away the Dodge brothers' free choice in the matter of whether or not to sell their shares.

It was, however, a Pyrrhic victory. The Dodge brothers used the proceeds of the forced sale to complete setting up their own automobile manufacturing company. They soon designed and marketed an automobile that many car enthusiasts still consider one of the best popular vehicles ever built, the 1926 Dodge. This made the venerable Model T Ford, the basic design of which Henry Ford had resisted changing for almost twenty years (1908-1927), obsolete. Henry Ford was forced to invest vast sums in developing a competitor to the Dodge product, and spent millions more retooling his factories to produce the Model A in 1928. His refusal to share power and pay dividends to minority shareholders cost Henry Ford a huge fortune, and ensured that his company lost its position as the world's leading automobile manufacturer.

Aside from the personal cost to Henry Ford, the social cost of *Dodge v. Ford Motor Company* was enormous. It embodied the attenuation of the property rights of minority shareholders into law, economic theory, and fiscal and monetary policy — and thus into the United States Internal Revenue Code. The consequences of this action were profound and far-reaching.

An owner has the natural right to the profits generated by what he or she owns. Denying this right, as Henry Ford did to the Dodge brothers, abolishes private property to that degree. The myth that capital formation is only financed out of past savings provides the justification for this undermining of a natural right. Two facts, however, contradict the myth of the necessity of existing accumulations of savings to finance new capital formation.

One, capital is not usually financed out of existing accumulations of savings — directly. The chief use of savings (which necessarily equals investment, as Keynes agreed, indeed, insisted on) is as collateral for debt financing. Henry Ford undermined the natural right to private property in two ways by accumulating cash to finance plant expansion: 1) he denied the Dodge brothers their fruits of ownership by withholding dividends, and 2) he violated the principle of sound finance embodied in the real bills doctrine, that money can be created without inflation or deflation if linked through private property to the present value of existing and future marketable goods and services. Ford thereby monopolized access to the means of acquiring and possessing private property.

Two, Henry Ford's chosen method of concentrating ownership — and thus power — in his own hands guaranteed that he would be accountable to no one for any of his actions. By concentrating ownership, Ford effectively negated others' right to be an owner, and actually went so far as to work to strip others not only of the rights of ownership, but of ownership itself.

While unacknowledged, *Dodge v. Ford Motor Company* helped set the stage for the Crash of 1929 and the current financial crisis. It did this by shifting the incentive for share ownership and the financing of growth through the issue of new shares. This changed from investment in anticipation of a future stream of dividends, to speculation in the value per share. "Investment" became redefined in the popular mind (and in that of many financial professionals) as buying and selling in anticipation of a rise or fall in the value per share, not in putting resources to work in a productive endeavor to generate income. The result was a near-total divorce of "investment" and share ownership from the revenue stream generated by profits of production.

Fortunately, just as the traditional rights of private property were eroded by a bad court decision, they can be restored by the stroke of a pen through reforms in our laws to encourage broad-based capital ownership. Since people's behavior naturally tends to follow the most advantageous course, people would soon reorient their investment strategy to conform to the restoration of the rights of property. The difficult part will be convincing lawmakers and academics that using retained earnings, either directly to finance capital formation or (more usually) as collateral to secure new money creation is contrary to sound finance and undermines the political stability of the State.

The fact is, while corporate finance is demonstrably not carried on in the manner described in academics' textbooks or by the nation's policymakers, such centers of influence and power continue to insist, contrary to absolutely certain historical and mathematical proof, that new capital formation is *always*, without exception, financed out of existing accumulations of savings.

Giving the lengthy proofs contradicting the dogmatic belief in the necessity of existing accumulations of savings to finance capital is outside the scope of this book, and would be a diversion in any event. The theoretical basis of financing new capital formation, the real bills doctrine, can be found in the work of (among others) Adam Smith (*The Wealth of Nations*, 1776), Henry Thornton (*An Enquiry into the Nature and Effects of the Paper Credit of Great Britain*, 1802), Jean-Baptiste Say (*Treatise on Po-*

litical Economy, 1821; *Letters to Mr. Malthus,* 1821), and John Fullarton (*Regulation of Currencies of the Bank of England,* 1844). Practical application and empirical proof can be found primarily in the work of Dr. Harold G. Moulton (chiefly *The Formation of Capital,* 1935), with corroboration and verification found in the work of Louis Kelso and Mortimer Adler (*The New Capitalists,* 1961). In this context, the subtitle of Kelso and Adler's book is significant: "A Proposal to Free Economic Growth from the Slavery of Savings."

The bottom line, of course, is that the mechanics of restoring the rights of private property are almost ridiculously easy, not to say straightforward and simple. The hard part is convincing academics and policymakers of the desirability of the only thing that has any hope of restoring a sound economy, and thus of maintaining a stable political order.

6. The Fourth Pillar

The fourth and final pillar of an economically just society is one that, as we have already seen, is omitted from every economic system in the world today: widespread direct ownership of the means of production, individually or in free association with others. Widespread ownership of the means of production is an absolute necessity if society is to survive economically, politically, and socially.

There are three reasons for this conclusion, all of which we will explain as briefly as possible. One, with respect to economics, as Louis Kelso and Mortimer Adler pointed out in *The Capitalist Manifesto*,[1] advancing technology (capital) is displacing human labor as the primary factor of production. Given that production equals income, the amount of income attributable to labor is declining relative to the amount of income attributable to capital.

The income attributable to labor and to capital goes by right of private property to the owners of labor and of capital, respectively. This results in a state of society in which most people own little or nothing in the way of capital. Lacking direct ownership of the primary means of production, most people have no natural means of generating an adequate and secure income as capital displaces their labor. This creates economic disequilibrium — instability — in society. The result is a seemingly inevitable cycle of boom and bust.

Two, with respect to politics, an economically unstable society is inevitably a politically unstable society. When they understand that economic chaos can undermine and, ultimately, destroy their power — if not their lives and their property — the economic and political elites either join forces, or one takes over the other. In either case they

---

[1] New York: Random House, 1958.

implement what the elites believe to be corrective measures, but which (as we have seen is the case with Keynesian economics) are based on erroneous beliefs and principles. The motive for these actions is rooted in the desire to maintain the wealth and power of the elite at acceptable levels. Consequently, the elite readily accedes to programs that promise (falsely) to redistribute the minimum of wealth necessary to restore economic equilibrium and maintain current concentrations of ownership of the means of production relatively intact.

The result is that, in order to maintain their right to and rights of private property, those currently in power undermine their own position by destroying the meaning of private property. This is what we saw in the case of Henry Ford's dispute with the Dodge brothers. As Belloc pointed out, as the self-defeating effort to retain current levels of power in the face of economic reality continues, capitalism transforms itself into the Servile State, the Servile State transforms itself into socialism, and socialism implodes of its own faulty principles. The economy returns to capitalism and the cycle starts all over again.

Three, the social order absolutely requires a stable economy and a strong juridical order: the rule of law. A stable economy only results from widespread direct ownership of the means of production, while the rule of law declines rapidly when economic conditions destabilize. As Belloc pointed out, "to control the production of wealth is to control human life itself. To refuse man the opportunity for the production of wealth is to refuse him the opportunity for life; and, in general, the way in which the production of wealth is by law permitted is the only way in which the citizens can legally exist."[2] Private property, whether in labor or in capital, links the human person in the closest possible manner to the productive process, and provides the only sound basis of and sound backing for the money supply, money being a derivative of production. The natural effects and activity of private property cannot

---

[2] *The Servile State, op. cit.*, 46.

be duplicated in any meaningful or material way by artificial State programs that rely on abolishing or unjustly inhibiting private property through redistribution of existing wealth, whether directly through taxation, or through manipulation of the money supply.

The necessity for a stable political and economic order to support the overall social order creates something of a paradox. As we saw in our previous discussion on the laws and characteristics of social justice, the constantly changing environment within which people carry out the business of daily life, that incredibly diverse interaction between individuals, groups, institutions, milieux, and so on, means that the social order itself can, in a sense, be described as "radically unstable." It is for this reason that the social order must have an absolutely solid economic and political foundation. The social order will otherwise not be able to carry out its function of providing the environment for and, when necessary, assisting people in the pursuit of happiness (acquiring and developing virtue). Our relationships and specific milieux can then change radically, even from moment to moment, for our need for underlying order and security, rooted in our nature, would be met.

In other words, as long as we can exercise control over our own lives, individually or in free association with others, our specific relationships can be as many and as varied as we like. Secure in an economically and politically stable social order, we can change these relationships — as we must — from moment to moment without harm and even with great benefit to ourselves, other individuals, groups, and the common good as a whole as we acquire and develop virtue, thereby becoming more fully human.

Private property is custom made as part of human nature itself to provide a foundation for a sound economic order and a stable political order. This is why the right to be an owner — the right *to* property — is believed to be a natural right, and thus absolute, that is, inherent in every single human being. As Dr. Heinrich Rommen explained, the implication of the universal prohibition against theft,

"'Thou shalt not steal' presupposes the institution of private property as pertaining to the natural law."[3]

Similarly, what an owner can do with what he or she owns — the rights *of* property — can be as many and as varied as our individual wants and needs and the demands of the common good. As long as we, by custom, tradition, or positive law do not define the exercise of property in any way that negates the underlying right to be an owner in the first place, we can tailor the specific rights of property in our society to optimize the benefits we receive — the "fruits of ownership" — under specific social conditions. The right to be an owner pertains to the natural law, but, as Rommen continued,

> . . . not, for example, the feudal property arrangements of the Middle Ages or the modern capitalist system. Since the natural law lays down general norms only, it is the function of the positive law to undertake the concrete, detailed regulation of real and personal property and to prescribe the formalities for conveyance of ownership.[4]

Here, then, is the reason why widespread direct ownership of the means of production is so important, and why we include expanded capital ownership as the critical "fourth pillar" of an economically just society. Private property is not the thing owned, but the natural right to be an owner, and the socially determined bundle of specific rights that define how owners can use what they own.

The right to be an owner is thus a part of human nature itself. It is an essential aspect of the dignity of the human person. When individuals, groups, or society as a whole prevent or inhibit any person or class of persons from exercising the right to be an owner and shut off or inhibit access to the means of acquiring and possessing private property, especially in the means of production, without

---

[3] *The Natural Law.* Indianapolis, Indiana: Liberty Fund, Inc., 1998, 59.
[4] *Ibid.*

just cause and without following due process, human dignity is offended at the deepest and most profound level.

The fact that the right to be an owner is part of the natural law is, in and of itself, sufficient to insist that every man, woman, and child have democratic access to the means of acquiring and possessing private property. We need no other justification. Even if the powers-that-be reject the natural law, however, there are overwhelming and irresistible "practical" reasons for implementing a program of expanded capital ownership at the earliest opportunity — and for creating the opportunity through acts of social justice if that opportunity does not occur naturally or in a timely manner.

This is because of two essential rights *of* property: *income* and *control*. These may be defined in different ways for different societies, depending on the wants and needs of the people who have joined together to form that society, specific conditions, and the demands of the common good. None of this changes the fact that the rights of private property in any society must include the effective right to enjoy the *income* generated by what is owned, and — even more critical — the right to *control* that which is owned. As Louis Kelso pointed out,

> It may be helpful to take note of what the concept "property" means in law and economics. It is an aggregate of the rights, powers and privileges, recognized by the laws of the nation, which an individual may possess with respect to various objects. Property is not the object owned, but the sum total of the "rights" which an individual may "own" in such an object. These in general include the rights of (1) possessing, (2) excluding others, (3) disposing or transferring, (4) using, (5) enjoying the fruits, profits, product or increase, and (6) of destroying or injuring, if the owner so desires. In a civilized society, these rights are only as effective as the laws which provide for their enforcement. The English common law, adopted into the fabric of American law, recognizes that the rights of property are subject to the limitations that

(1) things owned may not be so used as to injure others or the property of others, and

(2) that they may not be used in ways contrary to the general welfare of the people as a whole. From this definition of private property, a purely functional and practical understanding of the nature of property becomes clear.

Property in everyday life, is the right of *control*.[5]

Belloc believed that the restoration of private property in our society is made difficult if not impossible by the fact that people's attention has been diverted away from the importance of *control* over one's own life, to exaggerating the need for *security*, with security of *income* taking precedence. Of course, as Belloc did not fail to point out, the best and surest income security comes from direct ownership — control — of the means of production.

Still, many people have become convinced that, as long as the State "guarantees" an adequate level of income — regardless of the source — all will be well. Of course, the State can only guarantee a basic income for all by making serious inroads on private property, thereby undermining — attacking, really — essential human dignity. In today's society, however, only income (Keynesian "effective demand") matters, not the production that, per Say's Law of Markets, necessarily equals income.

A focus exclusively on income was the problem that Belloc saw with, *e.g.*, Major Douglas's "social credit" scheme.[6] Everything becomes secondary to the need to redistribute purchasing power, including our natural rights to life, liberty, property, and, especially, the "pursuit of happiness." This last is redefined to mean not the acquisition and development of virtue as the primary duty in our ongoing task of becoming more fully human, but solely an adequate provision for humanity's material needs: secu-

---

[5] Louis O. Kelso, "Karl Marx: The Almost Capitalist," *American Bar Association Journal*, March 1957.
[6] *The Restoration of Property, op. cit.*, 9.

rity of income. Security of income becomes the sole end of society and of State policy, even if the cost is the effective surrender of those natural rights that define us as persons, thereby rendering us slaves.

What humanity requires, however, is not a narrow focus on purchasing power as the solution to society's economic and political ills. Keeping in mind that Douglas, in point of fact, redefined private property in such a way as to abolish it, Belloc explained,

> Such schemes (notably the chief one, the Douglas Scheme) do not directly advance, nor are directly connected with the idea of *property*. They are only connected with the idea of *income*. They propose, especially the Douglas Scheme of credit, to restore purchasing power to the destitute masses of society ruined by industrial capitalism.

> That is exactly what a good distribution of property would also do; but a credit scheme could, in theory at least, do the thing at once and universally, while the restoration of property is unlikely to be achieved, and must, however successful, be a long business, spread over at least a couple of generations. Further, no restoration of property could be universal applying to the whole of society equally.[7]

We disagree with Belloc that the restoration of property can be neither universal nor accomplished with speed and facility. Very much the contrary, as we will presently demonstrate. Nevertheless, we find ourselves in full agreement with Belloc's belief that we must not allow ourselves to be diverted from the ultimate goal of restoring private property by being expedient and focusing all our efforts (or even most of them) on increasing individual income *directly* from the productive process by raising wages and fixed benefits, thereby succeeding only in increasing costs. Legitimate and secure income results from ownership of the means of production, whether that ownership is of labor or capital (ideally of both). Schemes that

---

[7] *Ibid.*

focus on income to the exclusion of all else necessarily undermine private property to one degree or another. They thereby end up being self-defeating if the goal is to foster respect for human dignity and reestablish economic freedom. This is consistent with the operation of social justice, in which the object is not to force the desired end result, but to make it possible to attain the desired end naturally. As Belloc stated,

> The object of those who think as I do in this matter is not to restore purchasing power but to restore economic freedom. It is true that there cannot be economic freedom without purchasing power and it is true that economic freedom varies in some degree directly with purchasing power; but it is not true that purchasing power is equivalent to economic freedom. A manager at $5000 a year who may get the sack at the caprice of his master has plenty of purchasing power, but he has not economic freedom.[8]

The problem that we will address in the rest of this book is how to overcome the debilitating effect of these erroneous assumptions — especially the crippling misdefinition of money and credit and the breaking of the direct private property link between money and production — and carry out a program that will restore private property in the most efficient and just manner possible.

To do otherwise is, frankly, to ignore reality. Ignoring reality is not only one definition of insanity, it is a certain recipe for defeat and disaster. As R. Buckminster Fuller commented in *Critical Path*,[9] "You never change things by fighting the existing reality. To change something, build a new model that makes the existing model obsolete."

---

[8] *Ibid.*, 9-10.
[9] New York: Saint Martin's Press, 1981.

7. The Myth of Savings

A 2010 article in the *Wall Street Journal* carried the panic-stricken headline, "Lending Falls at Epic Pace."[1] In other words, despite the continually trumpeted "recovery," there was an "epic" drop in the rate at which new capital was formed and old capital replaced. As a result, "The struggling U.S. banking industry remains a problem for policy makers eager for banks to lend again. Lawmakers on Capitol Hill and administration officials have pushed banks to lend, particularly in light of the billions in tax-payer aid injected into the financial industry over the past two years. Banking groups and their members counter that they are under pressure from regulators to be more prudent and that demand from struggling consumers and businesses is not there."[2] Evidently, not only are money, credit, and banking political issues in the worst sense of the term, the authorities evidently firmly believe that they can order banks to start lending without bothering to make the necessary changes in our institutions that would make it *possible* for banks to start lending.

Given such approaches to something that begs for the application of common sense, no wonder hopes for a true recovery are still ephemeral, even years later. As we concluded our discussion of the four pillars of an economically just society, we observe that, despite the obvious benefits to be obtained from a rapid expansion of direct ownership of the means of production, many people — Belloc among them — simply assumed and continue to assume that the task is hopeless, or nearly so. In consequence, people either throw in the towel, or redefine reality in order to try and get what they think they want. This is an activity in which the current crop of leaders seems to excel.

---

[1] Wednesday, February 24, 2010, A1.
[2] *Ibid.*

We can understand Belloc's pessimism, and even appreciate it to some extent. The problem is that Belloc made the same mistake as Chesterton in formulating the principles of distributism. Ironically, this is also the mistake made by the Keynesians, the Monetarists, the Austrians, and virtually every academic and policymaker for the past two hundred years and more. The mistake is twofold: 1) using the wrong definition of money (one that implicitly destroys the direct private property link between money and production), and 2) not recognizing the act of social justice. We have already covered the act of social justice in the chapter on the limited economic role for the State. Our concern in this chapter is the wrong definition of money and the conclusions that flow from it.

Using the wrong definition of money forces the inevitable — and incorrect — assumption that capital formation can only be financed out of existing accumulations of savings. This assumption is what we can call "the myth of savings," and which Kelso and Adler referred to as the slavery of past savings.

From the wrong definition of money flow all the bad assumptions that have destroyed private property for the great mass of people. A bad definition has convinced them that the only way to advance technologically is to have concentrated ownership of the means of production, whether that ownership is concentrated in a small group of private owners, or (preferably) the State. This, in turn, has further convinced many people that technological progress is evil, or is at least contrary to human nature. That being the case, everything beyond "human scale" must be broken up or destroyed in order to reestablish a more human society — and all because the financing of new or replacement capital is assumed to be tied irrevocably to the slavery of existing accumulations of savings.

This sounds as if the Just Third Way has an animus against savings, or even against humanity. Nothing could be further from the truth. What we oppose is the wrong definition of savings, a definition rooted in the wrong definition of money derived from the British Currency

School. This is a definition that raises almost insurmountable barriers against most people participating in the productive process in any meaningful or material way. As we have already seen, the Currency School's definition of money assumes an absolutist State. The Currency School denies essential human dignity by putting people at the service of money, rather than the other way around. In the same way, the Currency School assumes that production is a derivative of money and that "money" consists solely of coin, currency, and demand deposits (M_1). This completely reverses the natural order of things in which money is a derivative of production, and M_1 (some add M_2) is a derivative of money.

It is something of a toss-up whether we address the issue of savings or that of money first. Because savings seems to be better understood (or, at least, there seem to be fewer misconceptions about savings), we will begin with savings, even though the myths about savings are rooted in the wrong definition of money.

Nowhere is the damage done by the wrong definition of money — and thus of savings — more evident than in the belief that capital formation can only be financed by cutting consumption, saving, then investing. This has led to the adoption of what can only be called nonsensical and self-defeating principles by all the major schools of economics, and most of the minor ones as well, especially distributism. Belloc clearly — and unconsciously — presented this contradiction at the beginning of Chapter II of *The Restoration of Property*. As he declared,

> As we approach the problem of the restoration of property there are two main principles to be kept in mind: —
>
> (i) The first is that *any effort to restore the institution of property* (that is, re-establish a good distribution of property in a proletarian society such as ours has become) *can only be successful through a deliberate reversal of natural economic tendencies.*

(ii) The second is that *our effort will fail unless it be accompanied by regulation making for the preservation of private property, so much of it as shall have been restored.*

Both these principles are essential to success.[3]

The italics are Belloc's. We dealt with principle (ii) at some length in the "Introduction" to this book, so we only need to repeat the fact that Belloc got things backwards. You do not correct an injustice by committing an equal and opposite injustice, or, worse, out of revenge exact more than you consider your due. Instead, you organize with others in social justice and work to eliminate the injustice by removing whatever barriers exist to democratic and full participation in the common good. This is obvious once we look at the issue objectively.

Principle (i) is a horse of a different color. Believing that we "can only be successful through a deliberate reversal of natural economic tendencies" reveals an orientation directly at odds with reality — so much so that, unless we can get out of the cage this orientation builds around us (with, oftentimes, our enthusiastic consent and support), we will not be able to restore property . . . or anything else, for that matter. Boiled down to its essence, Belloc's statement is an astounding rejection of reality and so contrary to common sense that it almost takes a miracle to overcome.

Why do we say this? The statement, after all, seems innocuous enough. Economics has certain "tendencies" — laws — that in the current condition of society operate in a manner contrary to many people's individual good and the demands of the common good as a whole. The solution sounds equally innocuous: reverse these tendencies, and all will be well.

To his credit, Belloc did not take the "out" that if people would just be personally virtuous and think or believe in the "right" way, all would be well. Belloc specifically re-

---

[3] *The Restoration of Property, op. cit.,* 37.

jected the idea that "We must convert England to a right
religion before we can make Englishmen free."[4] As he
stated in no uncertain terms: "This obvious and radical
attitude, at the risk of paradox, I beg leave to challenge."[5]
Instead, he pointed out that practical corrective measures
must be implemented, and the work of "conversion" could
go on at the same time. This, however, still leaves the
problem of Belloc's belief that reversing economic tendencies could correct the situation.[6]

The problem is that these "economic tendencies" (of
which the laws of supply and demand are usually singled
out for special vituperation) are part of the nature of the
science of economics itself. They have been observed and
proved empirically time and again. Take them away or
reverse them (whatever you want to call it), and what is
left cannot be called "economics."

That much is obvious. You cannot change the definition
of something — that is, change a thing's substantial nature — and still claim that it remains the same thing. To
do so is simply to lie to yourself and others. To "reverse"
the meaning or operation of the laws of economics is to
shift the basis of economics from its own nature to something else, and then claim that you are not doing the very
thing you are doing.

It gets worse. Economics is a "social science." That
means that the nature of the science of economics is
firmly established on deductions from observed human
behavior, on which we base conclusions. Within our limited human perceptions, conclusions based on reason are
the only thing we have on which to base our understanding of the natural moral law. This is because human behavior is based on human nature, which in turn is based
on the nature of whatever ultimate reality or "first cause"
created human nature.

---

[4] *The Restoration of Property, op. cit.*, 62.
[5] *Ibid.*
[6] *Ibid.*, 63.

As a devout (some would say "fanatical") Catholic, Belloc defined this ultimate reality as the Christian God, and His Nature as the basis for the natural moral law . . . of which the science of economics is an application. Thus, what Belloc claimed *must* be done in order to succeed, is the very thing that can *never* be done by humanity — nor by God, either, for it would involve God in a contradiction. The one thing God cannot do is contradict or reverse Himself, that is, deny His own Nature.

Correcting Belloc's errors, however, is surprisingly easy once we have the key to unlock the cage into which so many of us seem willingly to have incarcerated ourselves. We find this key in how we understand the natural moral law. Belloc's quarrel with the laws of economics, shared by a great number of devout people of many faiths, is quickly resolved once we realize that the general norms of the natural law are . . . *general*. Particular applications of the general norms of the natural law, while they necessarily reflect the essential principle involved, can take an infinite number of forms. Some of these forms may have, over time, decayed or become inadequate to meet current needs. Some of them may have been inadequate from the very beginning.

This is because applications of the natural moral law can only take form within the institutional framework of the social order — the common good. When these institutions are flawed or inadequate, humanity's particular applications of the general norms of the natural law within those institutions will necessarily reflect these flaws and inadequacies, and function to the detriment of some or all.

When that happens, the proper course to follow in social justice is not to deny, reject, or "reverse" the general norm of the natural law. Instead, we are to organize with like-minded others, and carry out acts of social justice to restructure the institutions so that the particular applications of the natural law within those institutions can once again function to the benefit of everyone within that institution.

Thus, we cannot, for example, assert that the laws of supply and demand are evil because people are harmed by their current applications, and then attempt to deny, reject, or reverse them. Instead, we must examine the situation and determine *why* the laws of economics are not operating to the benefit of every participant in the common good. We must then take appropriate steps to correct the situation, not try and change reality.

There may, of course, be times when we must set aside the laws of economics, but only temporarily as an expedient in an emergency situation. For example, in a famine, the natural tendency is for the price of food to rise far beyond what people can afford to pay. The solution in social justice would be to arrange matters so that people can produce more food, bringing prices down naturally.

As we saw in our discussion of the characteristics of social justice, however, social justice takes time. In the interim, local authorities, even the State, can, as a temporary expedient, take over care of people's particular goods and impose rationing, price controls, and similar measures to keep people alive until the situation can be rectified. (Unfortunately, the temptation for those in authority is always to continue such measures long after they can be justified, as it gives them incredible power, but that is a different issue.)

It is not, however, all the laws of economics to which Belloc objected. He singled out one in particular as the root cause of the decay of private property as a widespread institution: the necessity of existing accumulations of savings to finance capital formation; the law of savings.

In a supremely ironic twist, however, this "myth of savings" *is not a law of economics*! The fixed belief of the absolute necessity of existing accumulations of savings is a tenet of the British Currency School, and is based on the Currency School's bad definition of money and credit. This is a definition that, as we have seen, rejects essential human dignity and personal sovereignty, and assumes State absolutism as a necessary and normal thing.

Belloc's argument is straightforward, and reflects the understanding of finance embodied in all the major schools of economics. We will quote it at some length because it gets to the heart of the matter — but keep in mind at all times that it is based on a false principle, that is, the wrong definition of money. Given the wrong definition, however, Belloc drew the logical conclusion (again, the italics are Belloc's):

The larger unit of capital will automatically be accumulated for a lesser proportionate reward than the smaller one. *This is an exceedingly important point which the earlier critics of Capitalism overlooked. It is a major cause in the disastrous swelling of large accumulations and corresponding disappearance of small property and economic freedom.*

Capital accumulates for a certain reward. Capital is created by saving out of production for the purposes of future production, and it will not be so accumulated by anyone, the individual owner nor the Communist State, save for some standard of remuneration. A certain measure of this reward sufficient to provide an accumulation of capital, produces what John Stuart Mill called "The Effective Desire of Accumulation," and we cannot do better than adopt this conventional term. Without "an effective desire for accumulation of Capital," either in the private citizen or in the direction of the Communist State, the stores of livelihood, the maintenance of instruments, and (of course) addition thereto will dwindle and fail, and wealth will decline. Men will not forgo a present for a future good save on terms of increment. Whether as individuals, as families or as governments, men will not deprive themselves of the immediate enjoyment of a sum of wealth for the sake of a future sum of wealth, unless the second is larger than the first. . . .

It is an error, as I have just said, to imagine that this factor is only present under Capitalism. It is necessarily present under Communism, or under well-divided

property, and indeed in any economic system whatsoever. . . .

Capital is accumulated with the purpose of future
production in excess of its present amount, and if such
addition were not expected, Capital would not be accumulated at all.[7]

The problem is that, insightful as Belloc's analysis may
be, *it is completely wrong.* It assumes as a given, as an
iron law of economics, of nature itself, that *capital formation is impossible until and unless consumption is reduced*
— that production derives from money in the form of accumulations of currency or currency substitutes, not that
money derives from the present value of existing production or from the present value of a reasonably anticipated
future stream of income from production of marketable
goods and services. Capital formation is best financed not
out of past cuts in consumption, but out of future increases in production!

A brief look at the facts reveals the falsity of the usual
assumption. We will not attempt to make the case against
Belloc's claim — although, admittedly, we are being un-
fair to Belloc to put it that way. He was simply repeating
what the experts told him, and what many people down to
the present day believe as firmly as once they did that the
sun revolves around the earth.

As we have already noted, the theoretical refutation of
the claim that capital formation can only be financed out
of existing accumulations of savings is found in the work
of Adam Smith, Henry Thornton, Jean-Baptiste Say,
Thomas Tooke and John Fullarton, among others. Let the
theoreticians argue with them. What we will review —
again, very briefly, for our purpose is not to prove the case
itself, but to report the proof, which you may then examine for yourself in the original sources — is the work of
Dr. Harold G. Moulton, whose empirical findings conclu-

---

[7] *The Restoration of Property, op. cit.,* 53-5.

sively disproved the dogma that the only way to finance capital formation is to cut consumption, save, then invest.

In 1934 and 1935, the Brookings Institution published four books detailing an alternative to the Keynesian New Deal. The New Deal, in the opinion of many, was simply a way of disguising socialism, and was pretty much ineffective in any event. Even some Keynesians are beginning to suggest that the New Deal did not bring the United States out of the Great Depression of the 1930s.[8] It was the increased demand for war material to supply the combatants in the Second World War that achieved that goal, as was also the case in 1915, bringing about full recovery from the Panic of 1907.[9]

Of the four-volume set, the most important (also the shortest) is the third book, *The Formation of Capital*. After recapping the situation described in the two previous volumes, *America's Capacity to Produce* (1934) and *America's Capacity to Consume* (1934), Moulton concluded that the Great Depression was not due to any inability to produce, or to consume what was produced. Instead, the problem was financing new production that, in accordance with Say's Law of Markets, would generate the income to consume what was produced. This Moulton formulated as "the economic dilemma":

THE NATURE OF THE DILEMMA

The dilemma may be summarily stated as follows: In order to accumulate money savings, we must decrease our expenditures for consumption; but in order to expand capital goods *profitably*, we must increase our expenditures for consumption. . . . Under the modern system of specialized production and exchange the pecuniary savings of individuals are in the main necessarily at the expense of consumption. If an individual with an income of $2,000 elects to save $500 he re-

---

[8] There was an earlier "Great Depression" from 1893-1898 following the "Panic of 1893."

[9] *The Formation of Capital*. Washington, DC: The Brookings Institution, 1935, 65.

duces his potential consumption by one-fourth. Moreover, the aggregate of individuals who make up society must in a given time period restrict aggregate consumption if funds are to be provided, out of savings, for additional capital construction.[10]

Belloc — or Keynes — could not have said it any better. To accumulate monetary savings requires that the saver be able to afford to cut consumption. Belloc, in fact, explained the same concept in similar terms: "Another way of putting it is to repeat the obvious truth that the margin for saving in the case of poor men is narrow, while that of rich men is wide. It is easier to save $25,000 a year out of $50,000 a year than to save $2500 a year out of $5000 a year. And out of $250 a year no man could save $125 (in England to-day) and keep alive."[11]

There is, however, something that neither Belloc nor Keynes (nor any other economist adhering to the tenets of the Currency School) considered. That is, if we cut consumption in order to accumulate money savings to finance capital formation, there will be no market for the goods and services we propose to produce! People will have cut consumption in order to save, thereby making new capital an unprofitable venture. The "economic dilemma" is that the very means by which the economists tell us we must finance new capital formation ensures that the capital will not be financed. As Moulton explained,

> When the managers of modern business corporations contemplate the expansion of capital goods they are forced to consider whether such capital will be profitable. They must begin to pay interest upon borrowed funds immediately and they must hold out the hope of relatively early dividends on stock investments. . . .

> Now the ability to earn interest or profits on new capital depends directly upon the ability to sell the goods which that new capital will produce, and this depends, in the main, upon an expansion in the ag-

---

[10] *Ibid.*, 28.
[11] *The Restoration of Property, op. cit.*, 55.

gregate demand of the people for consumption goods. . . . if the aggregate capital supply of a nation is to be steadily increased it is necessary that the demand for consumption goods expand in rough proportion to the increase in the supply of capital.[12]

To cut to the chase (and cut out several pages of Moulton's careful research and analysis), if we accept the dogma that we must cut consumption in order to finance new or replacement capital formation, every period of intense capital formation would *necessarily* be preceded by a period in which savings increased in roughly the same amount. . . thereby also removing the incentive for anyone to finance new capital formation!

Studying the economic history of the United States from 1830 to 1930, with special emphasis on the period from 1865 to 1930, however, Moulton discovered something astounding — at least to adherents of the Currency School. In no case between 1830 to 1930, a century that contained periods of the greatest industrial, agricultural, and commercial expansion in the history of the human race, were cycles of intense capital formation preceded by increased saving. Instead, directly contradicting the Currency School dogmatic assertion, in each and every case instances of intense capital formation were preceded by increased consumption! People were not *saving*, but *dissaving*!

The conclusion is inescapable. Financing new capital does not require cutting consumption in order to generate savings. Instead, new capital formation somehow requires that we use our savings to increase consumption, thereby creating the incentive to invest in new capital.

"But . . . but . . . but that's impossible!" the Currency School devotee sputters. "The money has to come from *somewhere*! And if not from cutting consumption and saving, then *where*?"

---

[12] *The Formation of Capital, op. cit.,* 29.

We agree. If we accept the definition of "money" used by the British Currency School, there is no way to finance capital formation except by cutting consumption and accumulating monetary savings before investing. Fortunately however, like Moulton, we do not accept the Currency School's limited and limiting definitions of money and savings. Released from that particular form of slavery, Moulton readily explained the source of the financing:

> Funds with which to finance new capital formation may be procured from the expansion of commercial bank loans and investments. In fact, new flotations of securities are not uncommonly financed — for considerable periods of time, pending their absorption by ultimate investors — by means of an expansion of commercial bank credit.[13]

Understanding how expanding commercial bank credit requires that we understand money and its necessary direct private property link to production — which is the subject of the next chapter in this book.

---

[13] *Ibid.*, 104.

8. The Money and Credit System

In the Virginia Declaration of Rights, adopted June 12, 1776, George Mason of Gunston Hall, who had been charged with drafting the piece, detailed those natural rights he considered most essential to enhancing and preserving the dignity of the human person. To paraphrase, these are life, freedom of association ("liberty"), access to the means of acquiring and possessing private property in the means of production, and acquiring and developing virtue ("pursuing happiness and safety"). Probably due to his discomfort with human chattel slavery (although another view is possible . . . and will not be discussed here), Thomas Jefferson omitted access to the means of acquiring and possessing private property in the means of production when he "borrowed" Mason's list for the Declaration of Independence of July 4, 1776, limiting himself to life, liberty, and the pursuit of happiness.

The only slavery with which we are concerned in this book, however, is the slavery of savings. We are not, of course, hostile to savings, any more than we are excusing human chattel slavery. Savings are absolutely essential to the financing of capital formation. What we object to (and to which, if you insist, we are irrevocably "hostile") are the fixed and erroneous beliefs that 1) "saving" can only be understood in terms of reducing current consumption, and 2) existing accumulations of savings are the sole source of financing for new capital formation, that is, the sole means of acquiring and possessing private property in the means of production.

Both of these beliefs are based on the wrong definition of money. This is a definition promulgated by the British Currency School and accepted as absolute dogma ever since. Even people who reject all other absolutes, and others who elevate it to the status of religious revelation accept this dogma. While it would probably be a much clearer presentation to refute one or the other of these erroneous beliefs individually, they are so intertwined that we are going to have to take them both on at once — and we can only do *that* by coming to a correct understanding of money.

John Maynard Keynes presented the most widespread — and incorrect — understanding of money in his *Treatise on Money* (1930). As he declared (without bothering to present any evidence to support his assertions),

> It is a peculiar characteristic of money contracts that it is the State or Community not only which enforces delivery, but also which decides what it is that must be delivered as a lawful or customary discharge of a contract which has been concluded in terms of the money-of-account. The State, therefore, comes in first of all as the authority of law which enforces the payment of the thing which corresponds to the name or description in the contract. But it comes in doubly when, in addition, it claims the right to determine and declare *what thing* corresponds to the name, and to vary its declaration from time to time — when, that is to say, it claims the right to re-edit the dictionary. This right is claimed by all modern States and has been so claimed for some four thousand years at least. It is when this stage in the evolution of Money has been reached that Knapp's Chartalism — the doctrine that money is peculiarly a creation of the State — is fully realized.[1]

We can reject this understanding of money without too much trouble. It is an unwarranted intrusion on freedom of association as well as the rights to and of private property to claim that people may not engage in contracts for any lawful or moral purpose without the explicit sanction of the State. Worse, there is no connection whatsoever between money and production in Keynes's analysis,

---

[1] John Maynard Keynes, *A Treatise on Money, Volume I: The Pure Theory of Money*. New York: Harcourt, Brace and Company, 1930, 4.

much less the essential direct private property link between money and production. Keynes's explanation is directly contrary to the natural moral law and constitutes a direct attack on human dignity.

The correct understanding of money is at once easier to grasp and much more useful.

Money is anything that is accepted in settlement of a debt. *Anything.* If two people agree, of their own free will, to enter into a contract to exchange items or claims on those items to which they attach value, why should the State have anything at all to say about the matter? As long as the matter is lawful, all parties to the contract are satisfied, and there has been no deception or fraud of any kind, there is no need for the State to be concerned. Money is the medium of exchange by means of which parties to a contract convey a private property right in the present value of existing or future marketable goods and services.

This, of course, assumes that the parties to the contract *have* a direct private property stake in whatever good or service they choose to exchange. That is, the parties have the right to dispose of the good or service as they will within the bounds of the common good. As we have already seen, the State's role is to keep order and maintain (though not necessarily provide) a "level playing field" so that everyone's rights are equally respected. As long as parties to a contract keep the peace and do not infringe on anyone's rights, the matter ends there without the State becoming involved.

The conveyance of value or a claim on the present value of production (the property right) belonging to the issuer — not society at large, as some would insist — of the money is the essence of money. The understanding of money employed by the Currency School confuses the vehicle, the *form* of the thing, with the substantial nature, the *essence*, of the thing. The definition of the Currency School thus embodies a triumph of form over substance. This serves only to disconnect money from the present value of existing and future marketable goods and services.

If this were an anthropological discussion of myth and belief, we would point out that the Currency School has fallen victim to "magical thinking." Magical thinking mistakes appearance (form) for substance (essential nature). This is the "law of similarity." There is also the magical belief that knowing something's "true name" allows you to manipulate that thing and control it absolutely (positivism). Thus, if the all-powerful, absolutist State "re-edits the dictionary" and declares that a thing is "money," than nothing else *can* be money . . . *right?*

Wrong. We've mentioned the work of Jean-Baptiste Say in previous chapters, usually in reference to his "Law of Markets," which is that supply generates its own demand, and demand its own supply, and his theoretical support for the real bills doctrine. The real bills doctrine is the basis for Dr. Harold Moulton's claim that capital formation can be financed without recourse to existing accumulations of savings. It is Say's explanation of the real bills doctrine that concerns us at this point, although the real bills doctrine is also an integral part of his Law of Markets through its application of the theory.

To begin, the real bills doctrine is the basic tenet of the British *Banking* School. In sharp contrast to the Currency School, the Banking School claims that "money" is anything by means of which two or more people convey value or a private property right, and thereby settle a debt or obligation. This understanding of money is embodied in the common law of England, as a glance at the definition of money in *Black's Law Dictionary* will reveal, and as any lawyer who took a course in bills and notes should be able to confirm.

The Banking School is called by that name because it recognizes that commercial banks are designed and intended to create money as needed in order to facilitate transfers of value among people as conveniently and as safely as possible. A commercial bank can turn anything that has a present value — a produced good or service or a future stream of income — into money. This present value can then be exchanged among individuals or groups until presented to the issuer for redemption.

To explain further, there are two basic kinds of banks, banks of deposit, and banks of issue (also called "banks of circulation"). Most economists and virtually all policy-makers do not understand banks of issue. They frequently assume that all banks are banks of deposit. That is, a "bank" to them is something that takes deposits and makes loans. Period.

Given this definition of "bank" — which is absolutely correct as the definition of the bank of deposit — it is impossible to make any loan for any purpose unless a saver has cut consumption, saved, and deposited his or her savings in the bank. The bank then lends out the savings, taking a fee for the purpose, and turns over the balance to the saver as his or her interest on savings. Common types of banks of deposit are savings and loans, credit unions, and investment banks. These institutions function exclusively as intermediaries between savers and borrowers.

A bank of issue, however, is a different type of institution. A bank of issue also takes deposits and makes loans . . . *and* issues promissory notes. A bank of issue thereby has the power not only to lend out what a saver has deposited, but also to accept bills by issuing promissory notes. The bank accepts a "real bill," that is, a bill or note backed by the present value of something, which bill a borrower brings to the bank of issue and temporarily "sells" (pledges) to the bank in return for a general promissory note drawn against the bank's ability to pay.

The borrower exchanges the promissory note for goods and services needed to complete the process of capital formation. Once the new capital becomes profitable, the borrower takes a portion of the profits generated by the capital, and uses it to buy back the lien from the bank, paying back the amount loaned plus a fee to compensate the bank for the use of the bank's good credit. The bank accepts the money, returns the lien, and cancels the amount of money equal to the original amount of the loan. The excess — the fee the bank received (usually called "interest") — is the bank's profit, which it uses to meet its own expenses and pay out dividends.

This is where something called "future savings" comes in. Previously we have been in the habit of using the terms "future" and "forced" savings interchangeably. "Forced savings" has a special meaning in Keynesian, Monetarist, and Austrian economics, however, so we will try and restrict ourselves to "future savings." (We will not get into the special meaning of "forced savings" here; our goal is to explain how the system should and, to a limited degree, does work, not to waste our time analyzing untenable theories from other economic systems.)

Even with respect to future savings, we need only note that the necessary equation of investment and savings is preserved by saving out of future income generated by the investment itself and used to repay the bank loan extended by a commercial bank, not in cutting current consumption, saving, then investing. This is a process that Keynes and others declared was impossible, but which, nevertheless, happens every day.

To counter the theory — fact, rather — of money creation and future savings on which the real bills doctrine is based, economic schools of thought based on the tenets of the British Currency School developed a special theory to explain the "multiplier effect." The primary purpose of Keynesian "money multiplier" idea is to discredit the real bills doctrine and Say's Law of Markets. It does neither.

Money multiplier theory presumably 1) explains away the power of a commercial bank to create money by issuing promissory notes in exchange for a lien on the present value of existing or future production of marketable goods and services, and 2) thereby undermines the real bills doctrine and Say's Law of Markets. Under the real bills doctrine, of course, which ties into Say's Law of Markets, a commercial bank can create any amount of money by accepting bills, as long as the money is backed by the present value of existing or future marketable goods and services. If there is a reserve requirement, the amount of money that can be created is limited by the reserve requirement.

For example, if a bank has $1,000 in reserves, and is subject to a 10% reserve requirement, it can accept bills and create money by issuing promissory notes up to the amount of $10,000. Most authorities today, however, claim that this is either possible but too dangerous (risky), or simply is not, or cannot, be done.

Instead, the Keynesian explanation for the potential expansion of the money supply under fractional reserve banking is asserted to be the result of the bank with $1,000 lending out $900, and retaining $100 in reserves, and $900 in cash to back the demand deposits.

The borrower spends the proceeds of the loan with a check, which is deposited in another bank. This increases the reserves of the second bank by $900. The second bank then loans out $810, retains $90 in reserves, and $810 in cash to back the demand deposits. The $810 is spent in the form of checks and deposited in yet a third bank. This process continues until the original $1,000 plus the $900 plus the $810, and so on, equals $10,000.

While this Keynesian explanation of the multiplier theory is in all the textbooks, it is completely wrong. It requires counting every unit of currency in the form of checks multiple times, relying essentially on the creation of "fictitious bills." The explanation ignores one glaringly obvious fact: that the $900 in the second bank, the $810 in the third bank, and so on, are not in the form of cash, but checks. Checks do not remain in the bank in which they are deposited, but instead are taken and presented to the bank on which the checks are drawn for payment. The bank on which the checks are drawn does not retain the reserves, but turns over the cash behind the demand deposit. The amount of money in the system does not increase at all, but regardless how many banks it passes through, remains at $1,000. As Dr. Harold Moulton pointed out, giving the example of an original loan in the amount of $100,000 discounted at 2% (a net of $98,000),

> If all the people receiving such checks in turn present them to this bank for deposit to their respective accounts, it is obvious that, while there would be an ever-shifting personnel among depositors, the total deposits would remain at $98,000.[2]

Just as obvious from Moulton's full explanation (found in Chapter VI of *The Formation of Capital*, "Commercial Banks and the Supply of Funds") is that it makes no difference whether one bank is involved in the process, or hundreds, even thousands. The result is the same.

The bottom line is that a bank of issue performs the invaluable service of creating money by accepting a borrower's bill in exchange for the bank's presumably good credit, accepted throughout the community. This substitutes the bank's general credit for the borrower's individual credit, which is generally not known or accepted beyond the borrower's limited circle. The bank's promissory notes can take the form of banknotes, demand deposits, commercial paper, or any other vehicle that is readily acceptable in trade and commerce ("bankers' acceptances"). These are, to all intents and purposes, "money," for they all convey a private property right in the present value of existing or future marketable goods and services, and can all be accepted in settlement of a debt. The money is created, used to form capital, and the capital generates the future savings necessary to repay the loan that created the money to finance the capital formation in the first place.

The most common type of bank of issue today is the commercial bank. Few if any banks of issue actually print their own banknotes any more. Instead, they create demand deposits. The end result is the same: an expansion of bank credit.

---

[2] *The Formation of Capital, op. cit.*, 80.

A recent development is the modern "non-bank bank," or "non-banking financial institution," of which finance companies and consumer credit card companies are the most common examples. While this is not universal (the category is only vaguely defined by government banking regulations) non-bank banks typically do not take deposits. Instead, they only create money for consumption purposes, backing the new money not with the present value of existing or future production, but with the borrower's presumed ability to repay the loan out of other income (production) not linked directly or indirectly to the new money. (Again, there are exceptions. A number of non-banking financial institutions such as factoring houses and leasing companies, serve legitimate commercial purposes. These, however, are — relative to the economic impact of consumer finance companies and consumer credit card companies — of minor importance.)

Credit extended by a bank of deposit is therefore sound, or a "good" use of credit in the sense that even if all loans made by the bank go bad and are not repaid, no holder in due course of a check or other obligation drawn on the bank will receive less than the face value of the obligation. This is because all demand deposits are — in theory — backed 100% by cash deposits, or, more accurately, cash and cash-equivalent securities. Credit extended by a bank of deposit has the potential to be a "bad" use of credit in the sense that, in the case of credit unions and savings and loans, the proceeds of the loans are usually for consumption. Loans by banks of deposit are not usually intended to finance capital formation, which capital can then be put into production, thereby generating the income necessary to repay the loan.

Credit extended by a bank of issue is (at least in theory) a "good" use of credit in both senses. All loans made by a commercial bank (again in theory) are backed 100% by liens on hard assets with a present value, and again with collateral — assets that can be seized to settle the debt if the assets which the loan financed prove to be worthless or otherwise fail to generate sufficient production to repay the loan. If a commercial bank is part of a central banking system, the loan is triply backed by the central bank's power to "rediscount" — that is, create money and purchase loans from commercial banks, thereby increasing the cash reserves of the commercial bank, preventing "runs" and stabilizing the currency.

Credit extended by non-bank banks is, as a general rule, a "bad" use of credit on all counts. (Again, we state this as a general thing, given the overwhelming character of the non-bank bank as focused on consumer credit, and excepting those non-banking financial institutions that fill legitimate industrial, commercial, and agricultural needs, linking their transactions directly to production or hard assets.) To be a "good " use of credit, a loan must 1) be extended only for properly vetted productive projects, thereby carrying within itself the capacity to repay the loan out of future production of marketable goods and services, and 2) be directly linked to that production by right of private property.

The bottom line is that a commercial bank is established on the assumption that the real bills doctrine is valid. That is (as the real bills doctrine states), it is possible to issue money in any amount without inflation or deflation — as long as the amount of money so issued is 1) directly linked to the present value of a productive project or existing inventories of marketable goods and services, 2) issued in an amount that does not exceed the present value of a productive project or existing inventories of marketable goods and services, and 3) repaid out of income generated by the capital investment itself. This last is what we call "future savings."

The real bills doctrine is based on the nature of money. Jean-Baptiste Say described this best in his exchange with the Reverend Thomas Malthus, who took the view of the Currency School as an absolute dogma. As Say explained the nature of money (and note the essential direct private property link between money and production),

Since the time of Adam Smith, political economists have agreed that we do not in reality buy the objects we consume, with the money or circulating coin which we pay for them. We must in the first place have bought this money itself by the sale of productions of our own. To the proprietor of the mines whence this money is obtained, it is a production with which he purchases such commodities as he may have occasion for: to all those into whose hands this money afterwards passes, it is only the price of the productions which they have themselves created by means of their lands, capital, or industry. In selling these, they exchange first their productions for money; and they afterwards exchange this money for objects of consumption. It is then in strict reality with their productions that they make their purchases; it is impossible for them to buy any articles whatever to a greater amount than that which they have produced either by themselves, or by means of their capitals and lands.[3]

The key concept in Say's analysis is that "It is then in strict reality with their productions that they make their purchases; it is impossible for them to buy any articles whatever to a greater amount than that which they have produced either by themselves, or by means of their capitals and lands." You can't consume more than you produce. Money is the vehicle by means of which my productions are exchanged for yours. As Louis Kelso clarified,

Money is not a part of the visible sector of the economy; people do not consume money. Money is not a physical factor of production, but rather a yardstick for measuring economic input, economic outtake and the relative values of the real goods and services of the economic world. Money provides a method of measuring obligations, rights, powers and privileges. It provides a means whereby certain individuals can

---

[3] Jean-Baptiste Say, *Letters to Mr. Malthus on Several Subjects of Political Economy and on the Cause of the Stagnation of Commerce.* London: Sherwood, Neely & Jones, 1821, 2.

accumulate claims against others, or against the economy as a whole, or against many economies. It is a system of symbols that many economists substitute for the visible sector and its productive enterprises, goods and services, thereby losing sight of the fact that a monetary system is a part only of the invisible sector of the economy, and that its adequacy can *only* be measured by its effect upon the visible sector.[4]

At this point some people might complain that we have inserted these particular quotes in a singularly large number of our writings. This is true. They then add that they heard us the first time, and there is no need to repeat ourselves. This is not true. People, especially academics and public policymakers, continue to act as if the tenets of the Currency School are absolute dogmas of whatever faith they hold. They seem insistent on the utterly unbelievable idea that consumers and the State can continue creating money backed by debt instead of production, and go on spending forever without having to produce anything. We therefore have no choice but to say the same things over again, try to explain them in new ways, and hope the message finally begins to sink in.

The problem, of course, becomes what to do about this situation. First, of course, we have to reeducate the public, academia, and policymakers to understand and accept a correct understanding of money. We must then implement reforms necessary to change the present debt-backed currency to an asset-backed currency. Finally, we must put money directly at the service of people (not the collectivist "*the* people," which always means "the State"), instead of maintaining the current arrangement that forces people to be at the service of money.

This requires that we make a close examination of the role of the central bank, the institution charged with regulating the currency in most countries.

---

[4] Louis O. Kelso, *Two-Factor Theory: The Economics of Reality.* New York: Random House, 1967, 54.

9. Central Banking

In the previous chapter we looked at the nature of money and credit. We saw how commercial banks (*i.e.*, banks of issue) can assist in creating money at need without inflation or deflation. Under the real bills doctrine of the British Banking School, and as Jean-Baptiste Say explained, this can be done as long as the amount of money created — bills accepted — does not exceed the present value of assets or projects a borrower brings to the bank for financing, and the borrower has a direct private property stake in the present value of whatever he or she pledges to the bank to back the newly created money.

We also looked briefly at banks of deposit, and how they do not have the power to create money. A bank of deposit can only lend out what savers have deposited. A bank of deposit cannot create money by accepting bills and issuing promissory notes as commercial banks are designed to do. Unfortunately, the major schools of economic thought — Keynesian, Monetarist, and Austrian — all make a fundamental and incorrect assumption, that banks of deposit are the only kind of bank; that no bank can (or, at least, should) create money. Only the State, presumably, has the authority and power to create money.

We did not, however, look at a third type of bank: the central bank. A central bank is, in practice, a hybrid institution. It is intended to serve as a bank of issue for commercial banks, and by default or through expedience usually serves as a bank of deposit for the State. In theory, a central bank need have no connection with the State at all, other than whatever charter is needed to assign the central bank the State's responsibility to regulate the currency and maintain ultimate State oversight of the task to ensure that contracts are kept and a level playing field is maintained. Again, in theory, a central bank can serve exclusively as a bank of issue for commercial banks, ensuring a uniform and stable currency and an adequate supply of money for the private sector, with the potential of allowing commercial banks to have 100% cash reserves behind all demand deposits and promissory notes.

Many people, notably Keynesians, Monetarists, and Austrians — anyone, in short, trapped within the paradigm of the British Currency School — confuse the distinction between a bank of deposit and a bank of issue. They therefore almost inevitably misunderstand the function of a central bank as a bank of issue for banks of issue. Properly run, a central bank should never create money except by accepting ("rediscounting") qualified loan paper from commercial banks or individual businesses in conformity with the real bills doctrine. This would ensure that the economy always has an adequate supply of money without inflation or deflation, the currency is uniform and always passes at par, and that the currency has a stable value.

Reserve requirements and how they function are another area of confusion for many people. To begin with, a commercial bank's notes and demand deposits are backed not by its cash reserves, but by the liens on the assets that the loans themselves financed. Reserves are there only to give added security, and to ensure that the bank's currency and demand deposits pass at par — that is, have the same value without a discount or premium — with all other currencies in the region.

In a perfect world, the only checks presented for payment at a commercial bank would be in payment of an outstanding loan. That, of course, is unrealistic. In the real world, vendors receiving checks and holders in due course, such as other commercial banks, expect to be able to exchange those checks for cash. Naturally, they cannot use their checks to redeem the loan obligations of the commercial bank, for they were not parties to the original transaction.

This requires that the commercial bank keep a certain percentage of assets on hand in the form of cash in order to redeem these checks. Ordinarily, not all of the checks drawn on the bank are presented at one time, any more than the full amount of demand deposits are expended at one time. Further, a significant proportion of the obligations of a commercial bank can be exchanged for those of other banks that the original bank collects in the course of business, while other obligations will be redeemed in the course of paying off loans. Under ordinary conditions, the demand for cash redemption for the obligations of a commercial bank is, consequently, relatively low compared to the total amount of obligations outstanding.

That being the case, a commercial bank only needs to hold a certain fraction of its assets in the form of cash or cash equivalents, for not all of the bank's obligations will be redeemed in cash at any one time. Instead, the commercial bank will redeem most of its own obligations by exchanging its obligations for those of other commercial banks, or accept those obligations in payment of loans extended by the bank. This is the rationale of "fractional reserve banking."

Obviously, one danger of fractional reserve banking is that a commercial bank might be required to redeem a greater amount of its obligations than it has cash on hand. A commercial bank's assets are primarily in the form of loans it has made. The bank cannot ordinarily hand those loans over to redeem one of its own promissory notes presented for redemption or checks presented for payment, except to the original borrower. Instead, a commercial bank that needs additional reserves can sell some of its loans to other commercial banks that have excess cash reserves, thereby keeping the bank liquid.

A central bank can serve as a clearinghouse for commercial banks engaged in buying and selling loans among themselves. This serves as a check against a "dirty trick" that Adam Smith related in *The Wealth of Nations*, where a larger bank or a consortium would drive a competitor out of business either by refusing to purchase any of its loans, or (worse) by accumulating the competitor's promissory notes ("hold them back") and, when they had enough to exceed the competitor's stated reserves, present them all at one time for payment, forcing the competitor into bankruptcy.

A central bank has a far more important function than offering commercial banks limited clearinghouse services, however. A central bank, like the commercial bank, has the power to create money by accepting bills and issuing promissory notes — but not from the public, only from commercial banks and, sometimes, individual businesses. (Again, this is the "pure theory." In practice, most central banks do have one customer other than commercial banks for which they can create money directly: the State. We will see presently why creating money for the State is a *very* bad idea.)

If the demand for cash becomes too great for a commercial bank to handle with its existing reserves, the commercial bank can immediately rediscount (sell) some of its loans to the central bank, thereby securing whatever amount of reserves are required to prevent a run on the bank. In fractional reserve banking, a commercial bank does not have to turn all of its loans into cash at once. It just has to have the ability to do so at need. Also (in theory) a commercial bank does not have to be bound by the artificial constraints of fractional reserve banking. If more reserves are needed, then the commercial bank need merely sell more of its loans to the central bank.

Thus, the idea of reserves is not to ensure that a commercial bank's promissory notes are fully backed by cash or government debt. The promissory notes are backed by liens on the assets financed by the loans made by the commercial bank. Reserves assure the holder in due course that he or she can use the promissory note to 1) redeem a loan obligation held by the issuing bank, 2) exchange the promissory note at face value within the community in trade, or 3) demand an equal amount of the official legal tender currency in exchange which necessarily passes at par with the commercial bank's promissory notes. A central bank is supposed to ensure that there will always be adequate reserves, and that those reserves are in the form of an asset-backed currency.

Unfortunately, what should be the case and what actually is the case are different things entirely. What often happens in more instances than not is that the State realizes it can force a central bank to create money to cover the State's deficits. This gives the illusion that the State and the central bank can somehow create wealth out of nothing. It is a highly feasible political move as well, because when the State can print money at will, it does not need to impose direct taxation to raise funds. The politicians can let the hidden tax of inflation handle the unpleasant task of tax collection, with private sector merchants instead of the central government taking the blame for the rising price level. The currency — and, of course, all cash and cash equivalent reserves — gradually (or quickly, depending on the greed or incompetence of the politicians) becomes backed by government debt instead of hard, private sector assets.

Reserves, however, must be in a form in which the public has full confidence. Traditionally this has been specie — gold and silver. Since the First World War, however, reserves have usually been in the form of promissory notes issued by a central bank and backed by government debt ("cash"), or government debt itself ("government securities"). As long as the issuing government is stable and has the power to collect taxes in the future to make good on its debt, the public will have confidence in the legal tender promissory notes and the government debt. As soon as people no longer have confidence in the government (such as when the government issues more promissory notes than the tax base can support), the currency — and the government — usually collapses.

The State must then take steps to reestablish a sound currency. Usually this is a two-step process: 1) restore reserves in the form of hard assets of some kind (again, gold and silver are usually preferred because most people are convinced they have a stable value), and 2) guarantee convertibility at par (face value) of the State's official legal tender promissory notes with the reserve currency. The reserve currency does not, however, need to be in the form of gold or silver. It is only necessary that the reserve currency represent hard assets with a value determined by the present value of existing and future production, not government debt.

Obviously, fractional cash reserves are, in a sense, a form of insurance. As such, there does not need to be 100% coverage, for there is rarely, if ever, a 100% demand to convert a commercial bank's promissory notes into the official legal tender currency. The problem of fractional reserve requirements, however, is that it puts an artificial and rather arbitrary (and often politically determined) limit on how many loans a commercial bank can make — regardless of the number of feasible projects that might be brought to the bank for financing. In a fractional reserve system, a commercial bank cannot make loans that cause reserves to fall below the required ratio.

Still, reserve requirements are a good idea — and one of the main reasons for having a central banking system or, if you prefer the more descriptive name of the institution in the United States, a reserve system to provide, if necessary, any amount of cash reserves at need. As the Federal Reserve System was originally designed to operate in the United States, a commercial bank had to keep a reasonable amount of reserves on hand in the form of cash, qualified loan paper, or government securities. A commercial bank in need of additional cash reserves could either "rent" excess reserves on deposit at the Federal Reserve, or rediscount some of its loans directly to the Federal Reserve and increase its reserves that way.

There is an almost inevitable political problem, however, with establishing a central bank. It is virtually impossible for a central bank to obtain a charter unless it agrees to serve as the State's primary or sole banking facility. This can be beneficial, for such a provision usually means that the promissory notes and demand deposits issued by the central bank are backed by the full faith and credit of the State. It becomes in the State's best interest not to debauch the currency or borrow beyond its immediate ability to repay within the current period.

More often, however, using the central bank as the State's exclusive or primary banking facility is the fast track to economic and financial perdition. Giving the State the keys to a money machine — or what the powers-that-be have the tendency to think is a money machine — is almost invariably a disaster. As Henry C. Adams pointed out more than a century ago,

> As self-government was secured through a struggle for mastery over the public purse, so must it be maintained through the exercise by the people of complete control over public expenditure. Money is the vital principle of the body politic; the public treasury is the heart of the state; control over public supplies means control over public affairs. Any method of procedure, therefore, by which a public servant can veil the true meaning of his acts, or which allows the government to enter upon any great enterprise without bringing the fact fairly to the knowledge of the public, must work against the realization of the constitutional idea. This is exactly the state of affairs introduced by a free use of public credit. Under ordinary circumstances, popular attention can not be drawn to public acts, except they touch the pocket of the voters through an increase in taxes; and it follows that a government whose expenditures are met by resort to loans may, for a time, administer affairs independently of those who must finally settle the account.[1]

This is why including government securities in the definition of reserves causes serious problems. It opens up a back door by means of which the State can, to all intents and purposes, print money at will. This is because in order to regulate reserve requirements of commercial banks, the central bank has to be able to buy and sell secondary

---

[1] *Public Debts, An Essay in the Science of Finance*. New York: D. Appleton and Company, 1898, 22-23.

government securities, that is, government securities that were sold by the treasury of the country to the public.

Thus, even if the central bank is strictly prohibited from dealing in primary government securities — that is, securities sold by the treasury of the country directly to the central bank — a government can circumvent this prohibition by passing the securities through the hands of intermediaries for a microsecond. This creates an extremely lucrative "triangle trade" in government debt for a few chosen individuals instead of monetizing deficits directly. The process transforms primary securities into secondary securities by sleight-of-hand.

The ease with which governments can hijack the purpose of a central bank and divert it to its own purposes argues a serious need for fundamental systemic reform. That is, the situation is ripe for acts of social justice directed at reforming the institution to conform more closely to the demands of the common good. Like the State itself, a central bank is a tool. If it is used in a manner contrary to the common good of all humanity, that is, the central bank works to inhibit or prevent the acquisition and development of virtue by the great mass of people, it must be reformed so that it serves its original purpose.

10. Own the Fed, Reform the IRS

In the previous chapter we concluded that if a central bank does not adequately serve the purpose for which it was invented, that is, the institution works so as to inhibit or prevent people from realizing their fullest potential as human beings, it must be reformed. Naturally enough, this raises the question as to the special role of a central bank — or any bank, for that matter.

Bank credit being the primary means by which people acquire ownership of the means of production, the need for reform of the central bank must be judged by how well it assists every individual in becoming a direct owner of a meaningful private property stake in income-generating assets. As we saw in Chapter 1 the right to be an owner is by definition inherent, that is natural or absolute, in every human being. This is critical, for ownership of the means of production is the chief means by which each person secures the right to life and liberty, and carries out the task of acquiring and developing virtue — pursuing happiness and safety. To put it more simply, direct ownership of the means of production is the principle support for basic human dignity, and should be recognized and protected as a fundamental right of citizenship.

Consistent with the principles of the Just Third Way, we believe that there are at least four reforms essential to restoring money, credit, and banking to their organic roots. These reforms would, we believe, bring these unique institutions back into conformity with the roles they are designed to fill, with special focus on the central bank.

Obviously, any reforms must be carried out in a manner consistent with human nature and the demands of the common good, and with ends in view that are equally consistent with nature. The necessary reforms are 1) a mandatory 100% reserve requirement for all commercial banks, 2) a "two-tiered" interest rate system, 3) widespread direct ownership of the means of production, and 4) direct shared ownership by all citizens of the central bank, the primary institution concerned with the means of acquiring and possessing private property, by every citizen.

The 100% Reserve Requirement

As we have seen, banks of deposit automatically back all of their deposits 100% with cash and sound, liquid securities. This is because a bank of deposit can only lend out what it takes in as a deposit. A bank of deposit cannot create money by issuing promissory notes and backing its demand deposits with liens on hard assets.

In theory, however, a commercial bank need not back its demand deposits with anything other than liens on hard assets. For security and to instill public confidence in a commercial bank, however, it is best to have a reserve requirement.

For this purpose, 100% cash reserves would be ideal. A 100% reserve requirement would give people 100% confidence in the commercial bank. A 100% reserve requirement can be implemented easily with only a few simple changes in the law, *e.g.*, mandating automatic rediscounting of all industrial, commercial, and agricultural loans and extending the term from the current traditional 90 days to one consistent with the financing period of the capital being purchased.

Ninety days is customary only because for centuries most commercial paper was issued for no more than 90 days. This was due to the fact that people in commerce generally saw no need to extend credit for any greater period of time, "settling day" coming at the end of every quarter.

There was a push to instate a 100% reserve requirement in the United States in the 1930s, headed by the brilliant Henry Simons, founder of the Chicago School of economics. Dr. Simons, however, used the definition of money coming from the British Currency School. Consequently, the "Chicago Plan," while it had limited potential to stop the abuses that contributed to the Crash of 1929, was essentially a reversion to the system established by the seriously flawed National Banking Act of 1863.

The proposal consisted largely of a recommendation to convert all banks of issue (commercial banks) into banks of deposit, including the Federal Reserve. This would remove the Federal Reserve's special character as a bank of issue for commercial banks, and prevent commercial banks from creating money through the issuance of promissory notes.[1]

One of the most serious flaws in the Chicago Plan as outlined by Simons was the fact that, in common with the National Banking Act of 1863 and the British Bank Charter Act of 1844 (on which the National Banking Act of 1863 was modeled), "reserves" were defined as cash and, behind the cash, government securities: debt.

A special monetary authority was to be appointed to determine the amount of money needed in the economy. The federal government would issue new debt to allow for any anticipated or necessary increase. Simons was never able to develop what he believed to be an effective means to prevent the State from seizing control of the process and using it to monetize its deficits.[2] Consequently, despite the urging of such diverse personalities as Irving Fisher and Father Charles Coughlin, Simons refused to endorse his own proposal or push for its implementation.[3]

The 100% reserve requirement under the Capital Homesteading proposal of the Just Third Way is materi-

---

[1] See Henry C. Simons, "A Positive Program for Laissez Faire," *Economic Policy for a Free Society*. Chicago, Illinois: The University of Chicago Press, 1947, 62.

[2] Henry C. Simons, "Rules versus Authorities in Monetary Policy," *Journal of Political Economy*, XLIV, No. 1 (February, 1936), 1-30.

[3] "Powerful Support Under Way For '100% Reserve Plan'," *The Wall Street Journal*, 02/19/35, 6.

ally different from Simons's Chicago Plan. First, Capital
Homesteading has a completely different orientation toward money creation. Under the tenets of the British
Currency School, money is presumed to be created first,
then savings and capital formation can take place. This
was the assumption embodied in the Chicago Plan. A
monetary authority would estimate the amount of money
needed in the economy, create it, and turn it over to the
banks to lend out. The sequence in money creation is presumed to be 1) create money, 2) cut consumption and
save, 3) locate a project or inventory of marketable goods
and services with present value, then 4) invest. As should
be obvious, there is a serious danger of either inflation or
deflation in this process if the monetary authority happens to guess incorrectly.

Under the tenets of the British Banking School and the
real bills doctrine, however, no money is or can be created
until and unless a potential borrower brings a financially
feasible project to the commercial bank in the form of a
bill and it is accepted. The present value of existing or
future marketable goods and services is determined, and
money is created by means of the issue of a promissory
note, then invested in the capital project, after which
money is taken out of the future stream of income and
used to repay the loan. The sequence is 1) locate a project
or inventory of marketable goods and services with present value, 2) accept the bill and create money to finance
the project in an amount no greater than the present
value of the project, 3) invest, and 4) save. As should be
equally obvious, there is no danger of either inflation or
deflation, as money can only be created as needed in response to the present value of existing and future marketable goods and services.

While this is the soundest method of creating money,
one thing more is needed. It is eminently feasible by using
a central bank properly in the way in which it was intended. Instead of having each commercial bank be liable
for its privately issued promissory notes, a central bank
can purchase all loans made by commercial banks to fi-

nance industrial, commercial, and agricultural projects that have been properly vetted and collateralized. Thus, just as an individual borrower exchanges his or her personal credit for the less risky and more acceptable institutional credit of a commercial bank, individual commercial banks would exchange their credit for that of the nation itself by rediscounting all loans at the central bank.

All new money would thus be direct issues of promissory notes not of individual commercial banks, but of the "über" commercial bank, the central bank of the entire country. All currency and demand deposits would automatically pass at par because all would, in effect, be promissory notes of the central bank. All promissory notes a borrower obtained from any commercial bank would be backed 100% by promissory notes issued by the central bank. This would institute an automatic 100% reserve requirement, achieved without the necessity of direct State control of the economy.

In conjunction with a 100% reserve requirement of this nature, the central bank would necessarily have to cease any and all "open market operations" in anything other than qualified private sector loan paper. That is, the central bank would not be permitted to hold government debt, whether issued by the government and sold directly to the central bank (primary securities) or "secondary securities" issued by the government and sold to the public and subsequently purchased by the central bank on the "open market." In effect, the central bank's role with respect to the State would be restricted to acting solely as a depository for State funds, and would not be able to issue promissory notes backed by government debt.

The Two-Tiered Interest Rate

As we have seen, the most damaging assumption of modern economics and finance, derived from an incorrect (or at least misleading) definition of money, is that capital formation can only be financed out of existing accumulations of savings. Given this assumption, a virtual obsession on the interest rate as the chief means for controlling the money supply and to induce savers to invest is only to be expected.

"Interest," of course, comes from *ownership* interest. It consists of the return due to an owner of a productive asset by right of private property. This causes problems because many people continue to insist, contrary to the evidence, that all capital formation is financed out of existing accumulations of savings.

Obviously, existing accumulations of savings have to belong to somebody. Given the underlying assumption of the necessity of existing savings to finance capital formation, then, one of two conclusions is inevitable. These conclusions become evident when people try to manipulate the system to ensure a just distribution of income, and they base their actions on the incorrect understanding of money and the role of savings.

One, since under justice an owner is due the income generated by what he or she owns, no one else, especially the State, has any claim whatsoever on the return to capital. The market alone sets the "interest rate" — the share of profits due to someone who provides financing out of an existing accumulation of savings. The interest rate is the market cost of capital. If someone does not have the wherewithal to become an owner of a meaningful stake of the means of production, it must be because he or she is lacking in some essential characteristic or virtue, and consequently can expect nothing.

Two, since the great mass of people have been economically disenfranchised by the concentration of ownership of the means of production, and the tenets of the British Currency School are accepted as virtual Holy Writ, then — so the reasoning appears to go — the principles of the natural moral law, especially liberty, private property, and the pursuit of happiness, cannot be absolute. They must be subject to modification in order to ensure that all human beings can share in the universal destination of all goods. This is the "generic right of dominion" inhering in each human person.

Both of these orientations are off base. Of the two, however, the latter is more damaging. This is because it at-
tacks and undermines the whole idea of the absolutes that
necessarily provide the foundation of the natural moral
law. The first orientation is that of capitalism, and widely
recognized by thoughtful people as being slightly "off,"
although most people assume that nothing better is possible. The second is that of socialism, and consequently
much more insidious, as it appears (at least on the sur-
face) to be more attuned and responsive to human wants
and needs. Nevertheless, socialism attempts to accomplish its end of equal or mandated results by overriding or
ignoring the basic precepts of the natural moral law. As
Heinrich Rommen pointed out, this leads to "pure moral
positivism, indeed to nihilism."[4]

The capitalists are right in this: that owners of existing
accumulations of savings are due a return on the investment of their savings commensurate with the market's
determination of the value of what the savings contributed to the production process. They are, however, wrong
in defining money and about the presumed necessity for
existing accumulations of savings to finance capital formation. The capitalist — or an all-powerful State — is not
as essential and irreplaceable in the process as the major
schools of economics would have us believe.

The socialists are right in this: that every human being
has a right by nature (the universal destination of all
goods; the generic right of dominion) to share in ownership of the means of production. Socialists do not, of
course, mean individual private ownership, but ownership
in common; they recognize property, but not *private* property. Misled by the false assumption of the necessity of
existing accumulations of savings to finance capital formation and an incorrect understanding of money, they are
wrong that the absolute principles of the natural moral
law cannot be regarded as absolutes.

---

[4] *The Natural Law, op. cit.,* 52.

Perhaps not surprisingly, the principles of the Just Third Way can be applied in a way to satisfy the expressed concerns of both capitalists and socialists. Obviously, an owner is due a just return for the use of his or her savings in the production process. We have discovered, however, that existing accumulations of savings are *not*, in fact, as necessary to finance capital formation as economic dogma would have us believe. Through the real bills doctrine, commercial banks backed up by the central bank can create money without the necessity of existing accumulations of savings. In *The Formation of Capital*, in fact, Dr. Harold Moulton proved that using existing accumulations of savings to finance capital formation has a detrimental effect on the capital financed out of existing accumulations of savings as well as the economy as a whole.[5]

The money created through the application of the real bills doctrine to finance capital formation is based not on existing savings owned by the *lender*, but on the present value of a productive project owned by the *borrower*. That being the case, it would be unjust for a lender to charge interest. The lender, after all, does not own the present value that backs the new money created by the loan. The lender does, however, have a lien, a legal claim, on the assets if the borrower fails to repay the money. All interest — profits or "ownership interest" — belongs not to the *lender* in that case, but by natural right to the *borrower*. The borrower is therefore due the full stream of profits or "interest." Thus, all the lender can justify is a service fee sufficient to compensate the commercial and central bank sufficient to cover costs and provide a just profit to the commercial bank, as well as a risk premium to insure against the chance of default.

A Just Third Way solution would thus be a "two-tiered" interest rate. The first "tier" would be set at the market cost of creating new money through the application of the real bills doctrine. This would be restricted exclusively to

---

[5] *The Formation of Capital, op. cit.*, 29.

new money. Consequently, all new money would only be created in response to qualified and properly vetted industrial, commercial, and agricultural capital projects — "blue chips" — and to monetize the present value of existing inventories of marketable goods and services.

Calling this first tier an "interest rate" is thus something of a misnomer. The money would actually be "interest free," both in the traditional sense of lacking a preexisting ownership interest, and the more common sense of a return due to the supplier of existing accumulations of savings. With zero-interest money (subject only to transaction costs and loan default insurance premiums), all profits would go to the owner of the present value of the asset being monetized. The credit would be "pure," unadulterated by the need to cut consumption in order to accumulate the savings necessary to repay the financing.

The second tier would be the market cost of money representing existing accumulations of savings. This would be for capital projects and other expenditures that did not meet the qualifications for pure credit financing. This would include speculative ventures, unproven technologies, and borrowing by individuals or groups with "bad credit." Also in this category — and probably accounting for the bulk of loans extended out of existing accumulations of savings — would be government borrowing, by nature nonproductive. Finally, consumer borrowing and most single-family home mortgages, as is the case today (in contrast to self-liquidating productive assets that pay for themselves from the future earnings of the acquired assets), would necessarily continue to come out of existing accumulations of savings. This would also be the case with reserves for all insurance and reinsurance pools, especially capital credit insurance, which, as we will see in a subsequent chapter, should replace the demand for traditional forms of collateral.[6]

---

[6] *The Capitalist Manifesto, op. cit.,* 243-244; *The New Capitalists, op. cit.,* 60-68.

Widespread Direct Ownership of Capital

The whole point of this book is to present the case for the restoration of property, and to examine a viable program to achieve this end. That being the case, a critical reform of the commercial banking system and the central bank is to ensure that all credit for new capital formation is extended and money created in ways that provide an equal future opportunity for all citizens, rich and poor alike, to gain meaningful ownership of the means of production as new capital is added and existing capital changes hands.

To be eligible for rediscounting, then, a loan made by a commercial bank must be made in such a way as to broaden ownership of capital. Unless a loan met this qualification, the borrower must go to the pool of existing savings. Given a mandatory 100% reserve requirement, a commercial bank could not issue a promissory note for an unqualified loan. The proceeds for non-qualified loans could only be taken out of savings deposited with the commercial bank.

Direct Citizen Ownership of the Central Bank

As we have already seen in this book, the best way to secure control over something is by means of the institution of private property. The obvious answer to the problem of monopoly control of the money-creating powers of the central bank by private interests or the State is therefore to vest direct ownership of the central bank in the citizens. This would, in effect, make the central bank a "fourth branch of government," structuring money power so that it would be directly and independently accountable to all citizens.

Direct citizen ownership of a central bank through equity shares with clearly defined rights attached — rather than the misleading socialist "ownership" in which everyone "owns" because the State owns — is the ultimate check on the potential for abuse and corruption on the part of the State. As civilization's only legitimate monopoly over all instruments of coercion, such systemic, "internal control" checks and balances are essential to protect and maintain the personal sovereignty of the citizens.

Commercial banks must continue to be privately owned. Ideally the customers would own these banks in the same way that they own cooperative banks such as credit unions, and savings and loans. This, however, is not as essential as direct citizen ownership of the institution charged with regulating the currency, the central bank. This is essential in order to remove the central bank from direct control of the State or State-appointed bureaucrats. This would provide an additional systemic check against the subversion of the "money machine" to buy votes and maintain a political or economic elite in power.

Every citizen, including newborns, through their parents or guardians, should therefore be issued a single, fully voting, fully participating, non-transferable share in the regional Federal Reserve or the equivalent in a particular country. As a right of citizenship, this share would necessarily be issued at no cost to the citizen. Similarly, when canceled upon death or transfer of citizenship, however, the shareholder's estate or the shareholder, respectively, would not be compensated for the value of the share.

There are a great many details that need to be worked out for a reform of central banking as it is carried out in the world today. There may be other necessary reforms to conform our money and credit institutions to the demands of the common good as well as our individual wants and needs. These, however, can be developed once the powers-that-be decide to grasp the nettle and deal with our economic problems in a serious and effective manner.

Reform the Tax System

Any way you look at it, the tax system in the United States is an abomination. Based on the tenets of the British Currency School, the tax system assumes as a given that existing accumulations of savings are essential to finance new capital formation and private sector economic growth. The tax system has been distorted, first, to encourage more savings and thus more investment by the rich, and, second, to encourage the non-rich to spend more than they make. The present federal tax system represents a virtually insurmountable barrier to widespread participation in capital ownership, democratic corporate governance, and the broad distribution of capital incomes from advancing technologies.

The Need for Tax Reform

Both changes virtually guarantee that new money will 1) be created in ways that concentrate ownership of the means of production, and 2) spur demand artificially by encouraging consumers and government at all levels to spend far beyond their incomes. In the latter case, the "toxic" home mortgage crisis was only the inevitable result of inducing the consumer to spend far more than he or she could ever hope to earn. Added to this, the non-mortgage consumer credit "industry" has the potential to maintain the current economic crisis or create a new, more severe one of its own.

To correct a situation that can only be described as inherently unjust and forestall a series of disasters even worse than the present one, we need to conform the tax system and the entire system of government finance and fiscal policy to support a restoration of property.

Coincident with this is the need to restructure the tax system so that it becomes possible for people to live within their means without the necessity of constant borrowing to generate artificially induced demand. Creating a vicious circle, "stimulating" consumer demand by increased consumer lending in turn justifies artificial job creation to produce marginally marketable goods and services — which requires increased consumer debt in order to clear those same goods and services at what can only be described as subsidized prices.

Saving Social Security

As a first step, we advocate eliminating the "payroll tax" and merging the Social Security and Medicare taxes into general tax revenues. This does not mean the elimination of Social Security and Medicare. All promises must be kept, paid out of general revenues, and kept per the original understanding and value of the promise. This is the basis of sound government as well as sound money.

Ending the payroll tax, however, would put an end to the nation's most regressive tax by increasing the standard exemption plus an essential minimum number of deductions, and only taxing income above that level — no exceptions. These exemptions plus deductions and deferrals would apply to all income from whatever source derived. The myriad of tax deductions, credits, and other "tax expenditures" would be eliminated, so that a family could fill its annual federal tax return on a postcard.

All promises that have been made must be kept. The government, however, needs to stop making new promises that it cannot keep, whether in the form of creating money to cover the increasing deficit, or refusal to reform the Social Security and Medicare system or other entitlements. These account for two-thirds of the Federal budget in "normal" times. This "social safety net" would then be properly understood as a supplement to wage and investment income instead of a primary source of income for so many.

Social Security and Medicare would gradually be phased out in their present form. They would be replaced by increased wage and capital incomes. The increased income would come from more rapid rates of sustainable or "green growth" of the productive economy, stimulated by the credit and tax reforms under the proposed Capital Homestead Act. For those below a very generous "poverty level," we would institute something along the lines of the "negative income tax" advocated by Milton Friedman. The amount would include vouchers for health insurance and education. Such a reform would also greatly reduce administrative costs for the federal, state, and local governments.

A Just, Single Rate Tax

We also advocate replacing the current progressive and regressive tax rates with a single rate tax. Social Security and Medicare taxes are possibly the most regressive taxes in history. They are levied on the first dollar of wage income whether the individual is making a million a year or is far below the poverty level. The single rate tax would therefore be levied on all personal income above the standard exemption plus deductions for health care and education. To this would be added a deferral for every citizen to begin to save and accumulate income-producing assets in a tax-sheltered vehicle called the Capital Homestead Account, or "CHA." Being "self-funded," CHAs would be an advance over today's Individual Retirement Accounts, or IRAs.

With guaranteed democratic access to capital credit for financially feasible projects, every citizen, whether or not he or she currently owns any capital in any form, would be empowered to purchase newly issued or transferred shares through his or her CHA administered by local banks, and repay the capital credit extended for the purchases out of the "future savings" made possible from the full distribution of profits on shares acquired by the newly economically enfranchised capital owners.

The Fed and the IRS

While no one at the time put the two concepts together, with the institution of the Federal Reserve System in 1913 (perhaps not coincidentally, the same year in which the income tax was established) it became possible for the first time in American history to have a coordinated and systematic program of creating interest-free "new money" in ways that would universalize access to capital ownership and break the dependency on existing accumulations of savings.

The twelve banks of the Federal Reserve System, although "hijacked" during World War I to finance government deficits and never returned to their original purpose, were intended to serve as regional development banks. They have the capacity under existing law to extend credit via the "discount window" through member commercial banks for qualified industrial, commercial, and agricultural investment.[7]

The shift away from the Federal Reserve System's stated purpose in providing a flexible and stable asset-backed currency by discounting private-sector productive loans to finance growth of agriculture, industry, and commerce, to a debt-backed currency to cover non-productive federal deficits, was made official in the 1930s. This was with the formation of the "Open Market Committee," headquartered at the Federal Reserve bank in New York City. Ironically, one of the chief reasons for the formation of the Federal Reserve System was to break the monopoly on money and credit held by Wall Street.[8]

With the institutionalization of open market operations via the Open Market Committee centered in New York City used to fund government deficits, the "money power" in the United States became even more concentrated than before the Panic of 1907. Ironically, the Panic resulted in the investigations that led to the formation of the Federal Reserve System.

Far from being key installations in a program to spread out economic power, the eleven Federal Reserve Banks outside New York have become relegated largely to research roles, and implementing policies dictated by the Federal Reserve Board of Governors in Washington, DC, and the Open Market Committee in New York.

At the same time that the Federal Reserve was being shifted from its primary task of providing liquidity for private sector growth and development, the income tax was transformed and its complexity increased beyond be-

---

[7] § 13 of the Federal Reserve Act of 1913.

[8] U.S. Congressional House Committee on Banking and Currency, *Report of the Committee Appointed Pursuant to House Resolutions 429 and 504 to Investigate the Concentration of Control of Money and Credit*. Washington, DC: U.S. Government Printing Office, 1913.

lief by the fixed idea that only existing accumulations of savings can be used to finance new capital formation. Consequently, the income tax has been complicated in ways to encourage people to save and provide the financing for new private sector capital. Thus, there has been a complete reversal of roles for the central bank and the tax system, all due to erroneous ideas about money, credit, banking, and private property.

A reform of both institutions represents a revolutionary restructuring of the Welfare State based on class warfare and redistribution, to a state of welfare based on the economic empowerment through capital ownership of every citizen as a fundamental right of citizenship and self-governance. This, of course, would make the State more dependent on the citizens, rather than having the citizens increasingly dependent on an absolutist government.

11. Enact a Capital Homestead Act

All of the measures discussed in the previous chapters in this book are, as we mentioned, part of a larger proposal with the name "Capital Homesteading." Capital Homesteading is a financially sound and politically feasible program to restore private property for the great mass of people in a manner consistent with the principles of the Just Third Way. It is thus in conformity with the demands of the common good and the dignity of the human person. How this can be done is (at least compared to the gyrations and complications of Keynesian economics) relatively simple.

Naturally we cannot give the complete Capital Homesteading program in a chapter or two. Even the "fleshed out" outline given in the book *Capital Homesteading for Every Citizen*[1] is a manual to guide policymakers and advisors to put together a specific legislative package. It is not a specific blueprint to detail every step that needs to be taken. Finally, the point of this book is to point the way to a restoration of private property, a goal that, strictly speaking, concerns only two of the four pillars of an economically just society that we listed earlier in this book, 3) restoration of the rights of private property, especially in corporate equity, and the "fatal omission," 4) widespread direct ownership of the means of production.

Not that these two pillars can be separated from the first two, 1) a limited economic role for the State, and 2) a free and open market as the best means for determining just wages, just prices, and just profits, in any realistic manner. If this book does nothing else, it will demonstrate that, even in this simplified presentation, all the elements of the Just Third Way are interconnected with and interdependent on all the others to a very high degree.

---

[1] Arlington, Virginia: Economic Justice Media, 2004.

This is directly analogous to how the institutions of the common good come together in a complex and inter-dependent network. Thus, isolating the elements of the Just Third Way even for the purposes of analysis and discussion is extremely difficult.

We cannot consider the restoration of property without also taking into account the role of the State and the market. To understand what needs to be done, we necessarily distinguish between the natural right *to* property of the means of production (the absolute right every human being has to be an owner, individually or in free association with others), from the socially determined rights *of* property. The rights *of* property are the specific institutions that define what an owner may do with what he or she owns, and often, for the sake of expedience, whether a specific thing (such as a nuclear bomb) should be private owned.

We must, therefore, keep current social and legal conditions in mind when considering the problem. To this we necessarily add all the principles of the Just Third Way as well as the basic precepts of the natural moral law and the laws of economics. Unless we fall into the trap of Machiavelli and start believing that the end justifies the means, we cannot take short cuts by redefining basic institutions, or by asserting that a particular expedient is good when we know full well — or should know, based on common sense — that it is really bad. On the contrary, we must keep all these things in mind without denigrating or dismissing any of them.

That being the case, we can present (at least in brief) the case for enacting a Capital Homestead Act.

As a first principle we take as a given that productive capacity must be restored. We can no longer adhere to the Keynesian dogma that it is possible to continue to redistribute and consume wealth without producing anything. That requires an examination of the system by means of which capital is financed and put to use, as well as the distributive mechanism inherent in the rights of private property.

In "normal" times in the United States, public and private productive capital grows annually at a rate of about $7,000 for every man, woman and child. This amount increases dramatically if we include replacement capital. This new and replaced capital, the source of America's capacity to produce in greater abundance than other economies, is almost inevitably financed in traditional ways. That is, financial institutions and other sources of capital credit assume as a given what we have already demonstrated is false: that capital formation is always financed out of existing accumulations of savings. Since the rich and the super-rich are the only people who can afford to save under this assumption, few, if any, new owners will be created. As a result, ownership of the means of production becomes increasingly concentrated.

Over the years this assumption — the "slavery of past savings" — that underpins traditional methods of corporate finance has resulted in policymakers' and academics' unthinking adherence to Keynesian dogma. This has led to an enormous and growing wealth gap. A rough estimate is that the wealthy top 10% in the United States own 90% of all directly held corporate stock. Most citizens do not have accumulated savings — if they have managed to save at all — sufficient to meet their household needs for more than a month or so. If a typical worker becomes disabled or loses his or her job, he or she has little or nothing in the way of income-generating investments. Most people are wholly dependent on jobs, welfare, or charity to meet their needs. The non-rich have no independent source of an adequate and secure income.

Capital Homesteading is designed to close this growing wealth gap through the restoration of private property in the means of production. It is intended to do so in a manner consistent with free enterprise values of private property, free market competition, and minimal government intervention with voluntary choices among producers and consumers. In other words, Capital Homesteading is designed to eliminate barriers so that the poor and non-rich can lift themselves up into capital ownership, without taking anything away from the rich except the monopoly the rich currently enjoy on future wealth acquisition. Like the "the Great American Desert" covered by Abraham Lincoln's Homestead Act of 1862, the Capital Homestead Act is oriented to an open frontier — the technology frontier. Unlike land, however, which is limited, the technology frontier need never be "closed." The opportunity to become an owner of a part of the technology frontier can and should be made equally accessible to everyone as a fundamental right of citizenship.

The Capital Homestead Act is a proposal to provide a package of integrated income, gift, retirement and inheritance tax reforms. This is combined with monetary policy changes and other structural improvements to national economic policy. These are designed to provide every citizen an equal opportunity to own, control, and share profits from productive capital. It does this by opening up democratic opportunity to obtain capital credit. Capital credit is the primary means by which new and replacement capital is financed in an advanced economy.

The political rationale behind the Capital Homestead Act is that there is no reason why those who already have capital (and thus collateral to qualify for additional capital loans) should have a monopoly or be the exclusive beneficiaries of the government's control over "social goods." The most important of these are money and credit because access to money and credit largely determines who will own future capital. A political democracy cannot rest comfortably and sustain itself on a foundation of government-supported economic plutocracy. Decentralized wealth would also counter the corrupting influences of concentrated wealth in campaign financing, and inhibit or even prevent the continuation or reformation of the "unholy trinity" of the federal government, the central bank, and Wall Street.

An essential premise of Capital Homesteading is that those who have no capital should have equal access to credit in order to acquire capital. This capital credit can be made available by the country's central bank — the Federal Reserve System — and allocated through local lenders for financing the capital needs of the productive economy. To address the growing wealth gap in market economies, Capital Homesteading would end the monopoly held by those who already have capital and thus collateral to qualify for capital loans. As we saw in the previous chapter on taxation, the belief that capital formation can only be financed out of existing accumulations of savings "forces" the State to grant favorable — and inherently unjust — tax treatment to the very rich. This is to encourage the rich to reinvest their capital earnings. This further concentrates ownership of the means of production, and lays the groundwork for an eventual State takeover of the economy. Ultimately this results in an unending pendulum swing between different degrees and forms of economic and social injustice.

As described in Louis Kelso and Mortimer Adler's two books, *The Capitalist Manifesto* (1958) and *The New Capitalists* (1961), the monetization of capital credit under Federal Reserve policy and reinforcement by loan default insurance as a substitute for traditional collateral would facilitate the implementation of Capital Homesteading. Capital Homesteading reforms would then enable every citizen to establish a tax-sheltered Capital Homestead Account (CHA) at a qualified local lending institution. A Capital Homestead Act would allow every citizen to purchase and accumulate dividend-yielding, full-voting shares to supplement retirement income. This would relieve the burden on Social Security as the aged population expands. As with most ESOPs ("Employee Stock [or Share] Ownership Plans") and in contrast to IRAs ("Individual Retirement Accounts"), the citizen would put up none of his own money. Through the Capital Homestead Act, each citizen would gain access to self-liquidating capital loans at low service charges to buy equity shares. These shares would be expected to recover their purchase price out of future pretax dividends paid out to the shareholder. The loan insurance, with premiums paid out of dividends, would cover the risk of default if the loan fails to be self-liquidating.

To encourage the issuance of new shares for meeting the financing needs of an enterprise, the double tax on corporate profits would be eliminated. This would, however, only apply to companies that sell full dividend payout, voting shares to CHAs, or extend these provisions to existing share issuances. To secure economic independence, each citizen would be sheltered from taxes on his or her CHA accumulations below $1,000,000, or an average of $10,000 per year for a centenarian.

Obviously, not everyone will live to be one hundred years old or be able to put $10,000 each year into his or her Capital Homestead Account. Some people will only be able to put in the amount of their annual capital credit allocation, estimated at $7,000. This, however, is expected to increase dramatically as our current slow- or no-growth economy regains its health. Others will take the opportunity to put existing accumulations into their CHAs, or inherit sufficient wealth to reach the tax-favored accumulation limit immediately, carrying forward the tax deferral until completely offset against future income. Ten thousand a year is simply a rough guess as to how much an average person might be able to put into a CHA each year when he or she does not have to worry about cutting consumption in order to save.

As noted, capital credit insurance and reinsurance would replace the usual demand for collateral for properly vetted capital loans that create new owners. All other loans, such as those on which the risk premium for an insurance policy would be prohibitive, loans for speculation, consumption, government expenditures, and owners who wish to retain sole ownership of their companies, would not qualify for capital credit insurance or for discounting at the central bank. Instead, such borrowers would have to go to the pool of existing savings.

We anticipate that this will benefit current savers immensely — and provide a lucrative replacement invest-

ment for the rich who will lose their monopoly on ownership of new capital. The primary benefit, of course, will
result from the fact that the federal government, unable
to monetize its deficits by selling "secondary" government
securities to the Federal Reserve by means of the fiction
of passing them through bond traders, will be forced to go
to existing accumulations of savings if it wishes to spend
more than it receives in tax revenues. This will drive up
the market cost of capital for existing accumulations of
savings, possibly into the double digits, thereby benefiting
people who invested their retirement savings in government bonds. This will have the added benefit of making
the interest-free credit available to companies that share
ownership increasingly attractive. It will also cause owners who want to retain sole ownership and total control to
rethink their position.

By far the best investment into which existing accumulations of savings can be put, however, will be capital
credit insurance and reinsurance. One of the first rules of
insurance is that you must never invest your insurance
pool in the same thing that you are insuring — a rule that
AIG "forgot" in their anxiety to cash in on the investment
bubble. Given that all — or virtually all — new capital
formed is financed in a way that creates new owners and
collateralized with capital credit insurance, the insurance
industry will likely do one of two things, probably both: 1)
specialize in specific industries and invest the insurance
or reinsurance pool in a diversified portfolio of securities
in other industries, and 2) invest a significant portion of
the insurance or reinsurance pool in government securities — although private sector securities are preferable.

Paradoxically, investing capital credit insurance and reinsurance pools in government bonds will ultimately back
the money supply with the full faith and credit of the
United States government — but in a manner far more
secure and financially sound than at present. Currently,
of course, the officially recognized money supply, M_1 (coin,
currency, demand deposits), or, depending on the authority, M_2 (M_1 plus household holdings of savings deposits,

small time deposits, and retail money market mutual funds) is backed almost 100% by federal government debt. There is a small amount in "United States Notes." These can be recognized by their red serial numbers and seals. These are "officially" backed by gold, but are rarely if ever seen in circulation, having been hoarded by collectors.

Under Capital Homesteading, the money supply would have several layers of backing, compared to the current one layer of government debt. First, of course, the currency and demand deposits would be backed by the liens taken by commercial banks on hard assets financed by extending credit to feasible and properly vetted capital investments. The liens themselves would be backed by the hard assets — level two. The third level would be the capital credit insurance policy, representing a claim on the insurance pool made up of existing accumulations of savings and government securities. The fourth level would be the capital credit reinsurance — that is, insurance on the insurance, which consists of a claim on the reinsurance pool composed of existing accumulations of savings and government securities. The federal government, backing the promissory notes issued by the Federal Reserve with its full faith and credit, would be the fifth level.

Thus, instead of Henry Simons's Chicago Plan in which the money supply would be backed directly by 100% reserves in the form of government securities (debt), the money supply would be backed by 500% reserves, of which less than 100% would be in the form of government securities, none of it directly.

To further promote CHAs, a "National Capital Credit Association" (NCCA) could be set up to facilitate and securitize capital acquisition loans. The NCCA could be owned and controlled by CHA lenders and citizens. It would package insured CHA loans, create software for helping lenders to scrutinize the feasibility of CHA loans, and set uniform standards for CHA insurers, reinsurers, and lenders.

The NCCA and competitors qualified by the Federal Reserve would then bundle and take these securitized CHA loans to the discount window of the regional Federal Reserve Bank. The Federal Reserve would treat these insured dividend-backed securities (DBSs) as it currently treats government debt paper, using them as a hard-asset backing for the currency. An added benefit would be that as the federal government pays down the national debt, all debt backing would be removed from the money supply. The result would be a stable, asset-backed "elastic" currency that could increase and decrease as the economy requires without inflation or deflation — exactly as the Federal Reserve was set up to provide in 1913.

That is the essence of the Capital Homestead Act. To get into greater detail, the Capital Homestead Act is designed to:

1) Generate millions of new private sector jobs by lifting ownership-concentrating Federal Reserve credit barriers in order to accelerate private sector growth linked to expanded ownership opportunities, at a zero rate of inflation.

2) Radically overhaul and simplify the federal tax system to eliminate budget deficits and ownership concentrating tax barriers through a single rate tax on all individual incomes from all sources above basic subsistence levels. Its tax reforms would:

a) eliminate payroll taxes on working Americans and their employers;

b) integrate corporate and personal income taxes; and

c) exempt from taxation the basic incomes of all citizens up to a level that allows them to meet their own subsistence needs and living expenses, while providing "safety net" vouchers for the poor.

A number of specific financing and ownership vehicles have been proposed to facilitate the implementation of a Capital Homesteading program. We've mentioned a number of these already, but it will be useful to recap.

The "Capital Homestead Account" or "CHA" is the primary tax-sheltered vehicle for the democratization of capital credit through local banks. It would enable every man, woman and child to accumulate wealth and receive dividend incomes from newly issued shares in new and growing companies, without being taxed on the accumulations (including property and shares gained through inheritance, savings, and arrangements like ESOPs, CSOPs and CLBs). In addition to serving as a source of capital credit for corporate workers, CHAs would also provide an ownership-building account for individuals who do not work for profit-making enterprises, such as school teachers, civil servants, military personnel, police, and health workers, and for individuals who have no remunerative employment, such as the disabled, the unemployed, homemakers and children.

The for-profit "Citizens Land Bank" or "CLB" (previously known as the "Community Investment Corporation" or "CIC") allows residents of a community to share in the control and profits associated with land planning and development.

The "Employee Stock (Share) Ownership Plan" or "ESOP" channels low-cost credit for financing the needs of business corporations, such as expansion, capitalization and ownership transfers. The ESOP links private sector workers to ownership shares and dividend incomes in the companies for which they work. Shares acquired on credit by worker-owners are paid for out of the future corporate profits they help to generate.

The "Consumer or Customer Stock Ownership Plan" or "CSOP" lets customers of utilities share in the governance and profitability of "natural monopolies." This includes industries such as telecommunications, water and power companies, mass-transit, and cable television.

Thus, Capital Homesteading is in no way "pie-in-the-sky" or otherwise unrealistic. Instead, it is, as we have seen, a much more rational and financially feasible way to run an economy than the current slapdash, panic-stricken crisis management that results from adherence to disproved Keynesian dogma.

Thus the Just Third Way, which avoids the fatal compromise with and acquiescence in socialism by starting with the correct definition of money, can offer more than a vague and contradictory "hope" that leaves us hopeless. As applied in Capital Homesteading, the principles of the Just Third Way offer specific recommendations that do not rely on turning over control (and thus property) to the State, but on restoring to people their dignity as human persons by securing to them the exercise of their natural rights to life, liberty, property, and the pursuit of happiness. In this way we can best heed the warning with which Alexis de Tocqueville closed the second volume of *Democracy in America*:

> The nations of our time cannot prevent the conditions of men from becoming equal, but it depends upon themselves whether the principle of equality is to lead them to servitude or freedom, to knowledge or barbarism, to prosperity or wretchedness.[2]

---

[2] "General Survey of the Subject," *Democracy in America, op. cit.*

Bibliography

Adams, Henry C., Public Debts: *An Essay in the Science of Finance*. New York: D. Appleton and Company, 1898.

Aristotle, *The Politics*. London, UK: Penguin Books, 1981.

Bagehot, Walter, *Lombard Street: A Description of the Money Market*. New York: Scribner, Armstrong, and Co., 1874.

Bagehot, Walter, *The English Constitution*. Brighton, UK: Sussex Academic Press, 1997.

Belloc, Hilaire, *An Essay on the Restoration of Property*. New York: Sheed and Ward, 1936.

Belloc, Hilaire, *The Servile State*. Indianapolis, Indiana: Liberty Fund, Inc., 1977.

Christy, David, *Cotton is King*. New York: Derby and Jackson, 1855.

Cobbett, William, *A History of the Protestant Reformation in England and Ireland*. Rockville, Illinois: TAN Books and Publishers, Inc., 1988.

Dicey, Albert Venn, *The Law of the Constitution*. Indianapolis, Indiana: Liberty Fund, Inc., 1982.

Ferree, Rev. William J., S.M., Ph.D., *Introduction to Social Justice*. Arlington, Virginia: Center for Economic and Social Justice, 1997.

Fullarton, John, *Regulation of Currencies of the Bank of England*. London: John Murray, Albemarle Street, 1845.

Hobbes, Thomas, *Leviathan, or, The Matter, Form, and Power of a Commonwealth Ecclesiastical and Civil*. London: Penguin Books, 1985.

Kelso, Louis O. and Adler, Mortimer J., *The Capitalist Manifesto*. New York: Random House, 1958.

Kelso, Louis O. and Adler, Mortimer J., *The New Capitalists*. New York: Random House, 1961.

Kelso, Louis O., *Two-Factor Theory: The Economics of Reality*. New York: Random House, 1967.

Keynes, John Maynard, *A Treatise on Money, Volume I: The Pure Theory of Money*. New York: Harcourt, Brace and Company, 1930.

Keynes, John Maynard, *The Economic Consequences of the Peace*. London: Penguin Books, 1971.

Keynes, John Maynard, *The General Theory of Employment, Interest, and Money.* New York: Harcourt Brace Jovanovich, Publishers, 1953.

Kindleberger, Charles P., Manias, *Panics, and Crashes: A History of Financial Crises.* New York: Harper Collins, Publishers, 1989.

Moulton, Harold G., *The Formation of Capital.* Washington, DC: The Brookings Institution, 1935.

Moulton, Harold G., *Capital Expansion, Employment, and Economic Stability.* Washington, DC: The Brookings Institutions, 1940.

Rommen, Heinrich, *The Natural Law.* Indianapolis, Indiana: Liberty Fund, Inc., 1998.

Say, Jean-Baptiste, *Letters to Mr. Malthus on Several Subjects of Political Economy and on the Cause of the Stagnation of Commerce.* London: Sherwood, Neely & Jones, 1821.

Say, Jean-Baptiste, *Treatise on Political Economy.* Philadelphia, Pennsylvania: Grigg and Elliot, 1836.

Simons, Henry C., *Economic Policy for a Free Society.* Chicago, Illinois: The University of Chicago Press, 1947.

Smith, Adam, *The Wealth of Nations.* Indianapolis, Indiana: Liberty Fund, Inc., 1981.

Thornton, Henry, *An Enquiry into the Nature and Effects of the Paper Credit of Great Britain.* London: George Allen & Unwin, Ltd., 1939.

Tocqueville, Alexis de, *Democracy in America.* New York: Alfred A. Knopf, 1994.

Index

Norman G. Kurland, *et al.*, *Capital Homesteading for Every Citizen* (2004). A "policy manual" for politicians and civic leaders interested in the essential natural law principles for establishing and maintaining a just economic and political order. 231 pp. ISBN 978-094499-700-0, **$18.00**.

Michael D. Greaney, *In Defense of Human Dignity* (2008). A collection of articles first published in *Social Justice Review*, the official journal of the Central Bureau of the Catholic Central Union of America, this book helps us understand why so much of what is proposed as remedies for today's social, political, and economic crises cannot work. 303 pp. ISBN 978-094499-702-4. **$20.00**.

Michael D. Greaney, *Supporting Life: The Case for a Pro-Life Economic Agenda* (2010). Is there a common political ground on which Pro-Life and Pro-Choice can meet? Yes — an economic proposal that has the potential to deliver a good life for everyone. 116 pp. ISBN 978-0-944997-05-5, **$10.00**.

Harold G. Moulton, *The Formation of Capital* (2010). Originally published in 1935 as the third volume in a four part series presenting an alternative to the Keynesian New Deal, Dr. Moulton's book shows how to finance new capital formation without first reducing consumption or cutting pay in order to finance widespread ownership of capital. 232 pp. ISBN 978-094499-708-6, **$20.00**.

William Cobbett, *The Emigrant's Guide* (1829). In the early 19th century, William Cobbett wrote a series of pamphlets to show the falsity of the stories that circulated about America, and giving advice to help people relocate to the "Land of Opportunity," where anyone could become an owner of income-generating property instead of a wage or welfare slave. 240 pp. ISBN 978-094499-701-7, **$20.00**.

A Plea for Peasant Proprietors

By William Thomas Thornton

During the Great Famine in Ireland (1846-1852), William Thornton (1813-1880), an English economist, proposed that unused land be purchased by the government and sold on credit to families that would put it into production. In this way funds spent on famine relief would be turned from an expenditure into an investment, jobs would be created, and the benefits of widespread capital ownership would accrue to individuals, families and the nation.

Although never adopted, later thinkers, offering a principled, growth-oriented approach for the 21st Century, refined Thornton's vision. As the global economy experiences ever-more-frequent downturns (with accelerating replacement of human labor by advanced technology, reinforced by flawed methods of finance that concentrate capital ownership in fewer and fewer hands) Thornton's book shines light on the path out of today's global dilemma.

Originally published in 1848, this newly annotated and indexed edition of *A Plea for Peasant Proprietors* was prepared from Thornton's 1874 revision includes a foreword that examines a new framework for solving the global financial crisis, financing economic growth and enabling every citizen to become an owner of productive capital, as well as appendices explaining topical references and the political and economic environment within which Thornton worked.

364 pp. ISBN 978-094499-710-9 **$25.00**

Center for Economic and Social Justice

The Center for Economic and Social Justice (CESJ), established in 1984, promotes a free enterprise approach to global economic justice through expanded capital ownership. CESJ is a non-profit, non-partisan, ecumenical, all-volunteer organization with an educational and research mission.

CESJ's global membership shares a common set of moral values and works together toward a common purpose, transforming good ideas into effective action.

Building upon the ideals of the American Revolution — which was really a "New World" revolution to spread political democracy globally — CESJ focuses on extending economic empowerment to all. Going beyond the mere rhetoric of empowerment, CESJ has developed a common-sense, comprehensive plan — the Capital Homestead Act — to liberate every person economically. To build equity with efficiency at the workplace, CESJ has developed a management system for corporations of the 21st Century known as "Justice-Based Management."

CESJ's macro- and micro-economic concepts and applications are derived from the economic theories and principles of economic justice developed by the late lawyer-economist Louis Kelso and the Aristotelian philosopher Mortimer Adler. Combined with the ideas of Social Justice developed by Pius XI and refined by one of CESJ's founders, the late philosopher Rev. William Ferree, these ideas offer a new paradigm for the world of the 21st Century. We call this new paradigm — which transcends the power- and ownership-concentrating wage systems of traditional capitalism and traditional socialism — "the Just Third Way."

http://www.cesj.org

CPSIA information can be obtained at www.ICGtesting.com
Printed in the USA
BVOW020355040912

299389BV00001B/6/P